An Artist in the Rigging

AN ARTIST IN THE RIGGING:
The Early Work of Herman Melville

William B. Dillingham

UNIVERSITY OF GEORGIA PRESS, ATHENS

Library of Congress Catalogue Card Number: 79–156038
International Standard Book Number: 0–8203–0276–7

The University of Georgia Press, Athens 30601

Printed in the United States of America
by Heritage Printers, Inc.
Charlotte, N. C. 28202

Special Acknowledgment

The last two verses of Emily Dickinson's "I had been hungry, all the
Years—" are reprinted by permission of the publishers and the Trustees
of Amherst College from Thomas H. Johnson, editor, *The Poems of
Emily Dickinson*, Cambridge, Massachusetts: The Belknap Press of
Harvard University Press, copyright 1951, 1955, by the President and
Fellows of Harvard College.

For
Bookie and Hap
Cum amore et in memoriam solis marisque

TABLE OF CONTENTS

CONTENTS

Acknowledgments

For suggestions and encouragement I am particularly indebted to Janice Edens Mobley and Floyd C. Watkins. At a crucial stage in the writing of this book Emory University relieved me of all teaching duties for the greater part of a year. For this generosity and for the warm support of Frank Manley, then chairman of the Department of English, I am most grateful. In preparing the manuscript, I was awarded a grant from the Emory University Research Committee. Of the numerous excellent treatments of Melville's work, one in particular, *Symbolism and American Literature* by Charles Feidelson, Jr., has inspired me through the years, influenced my thinking, and served as an enduring example of what a work of criticism ought to be.

W. B. D.

A Note on Texts

Throughout this book, page references to *Typee, Omoo, Mardi, Redburn,* and *White-Jacket* are to the Northwestern-Newberry Edition of *The Writings of Herman Melville* (Vols. 1-5), ed. Harrison Hayford, Hershel Parker, and G. Thomas Tanselle (Evanston and Chicago, 1968–1970). Eventually all of Melville's works will appear in this definitive edition. Meanwhile I have used the most reliable texts available of works published after *White-Jacket*. These editions are mentioned in footnotes where references appear.

An Artist in the Rigging

To distinguish such a mariner
from those who merely *"hand, reef, and steer,"*
that is, run aloft, furl sails,
haul ropes, and stand at the wheel,
they say he is *"a sailor-man;"*
which means that he not only knows
how to reef a topsail,
but is an artist in the rigging.

Redburn

LEE SHORE
AND HOWLING INFINITE

Chapter 1

When he was forty-seven, Nathaniel Hawthorne published a collection of short stories, some of which were the products of his earliest years as a writer. In his preface he quarreled with obvious flaws, but he was at the same time startled that the stories expressed so clearly what he had in later life come to feel strongly. "In youth," he concluded, "men are apt to write more wisely than they really know or feel; and the remainder of life may be not idly spent in realizing and convincing themselves of the wisdom which they uttered long ago."[1]

When Hawthorne wrote those words his neighbor in the Berkshires, Herman Melville, had himself already completed a considerable body of early work—five novels—and in that year, 1851, published his masterpiece, *Moby-Dick*. The five novels that precede *Moby-Dick—Typee* (1846), *Omoo* (1847), *Mardi* (1849), *Redburn* (1849), and *White-Jacket* (1850)—are the subject of this

---

1. Preface to *The Snow-Image and Other Twice-Told Tales, The Works of Nathaniel Hawthorne* (Boston, 1883), III, 388.

book. They illustrate the validity of Hawthorne's remark as well perhaps as the early work of any writer in American literature.

It is highly unlikely, however, that Melville realized how wisely he wrote in those five books. A few months before Hawthorne published his comment on the wisdom of youthful writing, Melville wrote him, partly in jest and partly in disgust, that his own reputation was "horrible" because he was known only (through *Typee* and *Omoo*) as the "man who lived among the cannibals."[2] When he finished *Redburn* and *White-Jacket*, he wrote his father-in-law, Lemuel Shaw: "They are two *jobs*, which I have done for money—being forced to it, as other men are to sawing wood."[3]

Melville's disparaging remarks notwithstanding, Hawthorne's words ring true. None of Melville's first five books is, of course, comparable to *Moby-Dick*, but to study them closely is to see that monumental novel in richer perspective. Actually there is little in *Moby-Dick* that is new to Melville's writing. The early works, then, are extremely important as preparations for his greatest novel, but they are infinitely more than apprentice works. They are finished works of art which would have assured Melville a considerable reputation even had he written nothing more.

During the five short years that Melville was writing these five books his mind was a seething caldron of ideas and recollected experience. He got much of this down on paper, but not in stages of progressive philosophical complexity or artistic sophistication. Like many great writers Melville's creative electricity was on alternating rather than on direct current. The most profitable way of examining his early work, therefore, is not chronologically. One could probably learn just as much about Melville's creative imagination by starting with *White-Jacket* and working backward as by starting with *Typee* and working forward chronologically. Ultimately each one of the five novels has to be examined individually and judged on its own merits. Certain relationships are

2. *The Letters of Herman Melville*, ed. Merrell R. Davis and William H. Gilman (New Haven, 1960), p. 130.

3. Ibid., p. 91.

present, however; and they are best seen without regard to the order of composition and publication. Based upon those relationships, the organization of this book is meant to suggest a way of looking at the early novels especially in terms of themes.

Moby-Dick is both the outgrowth of Melville's early work and a mirror of it. Chapter 23, "The Lee Shore," expresses with such clarity and economy the principal subjects of the first five novels that I quote it in its entirety:

Some chapters back, one Bulkington was spoken of, a tall new-landed mariner, encountered in New Bedford at the inn.

While on that shivering winter's night, the Pequod thrust her vindictive bows into the cold malicious waves, who should I see standing at her helm but Bulkington! I looked with sympathetic awe and fearfulness upon the man, who in mid-winter just landed from a four years' dangerous voyage, could so unrestingly push off again for still another tempestuous term. The land seemed scorching to his feet. Wonderfullest things are ever the unmentionable; deep memories yield no epitaphs; this six-inch chapter is the stoneless grave of Bulkington. Let me only say that it fared with him as with the storm-tossed ship, that miserably drives along the leeward land. The port would fain give succor; the port is pitiful; in the port is safety, comfort, hearthstone, supper, warm blankets, friends, all that's kind to our mortalities. But in that gale, the port, the land, is that ship's direst jeopardy; she must fly all hospitality; one touch of land though it but graze the keel, would make her shudder through and through. With all her might she crowds all sail off shore; in so doing, fights 'gainst the very winds that fain would blow her homeward; seeks all the lashed sea's landlessness again; for refuge's sake forlornly rushing into peril; her only friend her bitterest foe!

Know ye, now, Bulkington? Glimpses do ye seem to see of that mortally intolerable truth; that all deep, earnest thinking is but the intrepid effort of the soul to keep the open independence of her sea; while the wildest winds of heaven and earth conspire to cast her on the treacherous, slavish shore?

But as in landlessness alone resides the highest truth, shoreless, indefinite as God—so, better is it to perish in that howling infinite, than be ingloriously dashed upon the lee, even if that were safety!

3

For worm-like, then, oh! who would craven crawl to land! Terrors
of the terrible! is all this agony so vain? Take heart, take heart, O
Bulkington! Bear thee grimly, demigod! Up from the spray of
thy ocean-perishing—straight up, leaps thy apotheosis![4]

Using the metaphors of sea and land, "The Lee Shore" focuses
on three basic ideas: the nature of experience ("the howling infinite"), the thirst for psychological freedom ("the open independence of . . . sea"), and the paradox of Promethean heroism
("Up from . . . thy ocean-perishing . . . leaps thy apotheosis").
These are the themes of *Typee, Omoo, Redburn*, and *White-
Jacket*. Disregarding the chronological order of publication, I have
linked *Typee* with *Redburn* because they deal centrally with the
nature of experience, and *White-Jacket* with *Omoo* since they
depict the hero in the act of acquiring and proving his independence. *Mardi* was Melville's third book, but it is the most ambitious
by far of his early work. Indeed, it may well be the most ambitious
of all his works. In a treatment of these three themes *Mardi* logi-
cally belongs at the end because it is the most comprehensive. It
attempts to do essentially what *Moby-Dick* does—to treat all three
themes in profound depth. It falls short of *Moby-Dick*, but the
scope of the attempt is obvious. It belongs at the conclusion of this
study also because it is the only one of the five books that shows
the emergence of the Promethean hero and that deals with the
paradox which Ishmael expresses at the end of "The Lee Shore."

The concept of experience as revealed in *Typee* and *Redburn* is
based principally upon the assumption that reality is not static but
dynamic and thus ultimately unknowable, "indefinite as God."
The howling infinite is perilous largely because it is movement,
whereas the lee shore of delusion and self-deceit, the comfortable
but ignoble state of unquestioning existence, is non-movement. The
narrator-heroes of these two books both are determined to *move*,
but neither is prepared for the consequences. Tommo never

4. *Moby-Dick*, ed. Harrison Hayford and Hershel Parker (New York,
1967), pp. 97-98.

4

gets used to the fact that he cannot move backward, cannot re-experience. Each moment is a new experience with no possibility for returning. Young Redburn has no desire to return to some previous state of happiness. From childhood on, he looks forward, not backward; he hungers for the new worlds that he vividly imagines. But he learns that anticipation and actual experience are widely disparate; the imagination is an inadequate guide to the moving world.

There are no adequate guides in the howling infinite. The highest virtue is independence from those things which pretend to be guides. *White-Jacket* and *Omoo* direct themselves to the threat of personal ties and the problem of acquiring and retaining independence. In *White-Jacket* the young hero finds it extremely painful to sever his ties, especially with his family, and to exist, as Ishmael puts it, "in landlessness alone." Both *White-Jacket* and *Omoo* include characters who represent the alternatives to landlessness: men who are shallow or corrupt. Melville distinguishes between such men and his heroes by use of the terms "manhood" in *White-Jacket* and "sailor" in *Omoo* to refer to that state in which dignity through independence has been reached. In *White-Jacket* the hero is seen in the process of acquiring it, of cutting away all tethers with the lee shore. In *Omoo* the hero must prove the durability of his independence while in the company of the lee shore's arch-ambassador, Long Ghost.

From first acquaintance with the nature of experience in *Typee* and *Redburn* to the acquisition and testing of personal independence in *White-Jacket* and *Omoo*, the young hero of Melville's early work moves toward "apotheosis" in *Mardi*. "Up from the spray of thy ocean-perishing," says Ishmael about Bulkington, "straight up, leaps thy apotheosis!" The term suggests glorification and transcendence, but for Melville it also meant inevitable madness and destruction. Taji in *Mardi* is the forerunner of Ahab and like him achieves extraordinary stature through perishing in the howling infinite. Their nobility is reflected in their destruction, for they pit themselves boldly against the "wildest winds of heaven and earth," and for that they have Melville's admiration. For a time they lift themselves to Promethean heights. Their greatness, however, is ambiguous and flawed, for the undeviating and futile search twists, distorts, and dehumanizes the searcher while at the same time raising him above the level of ordinary beings.

Although Melville's concept of apotheosis is also a theory of tragedy, the positive—or optimistic—side of it is obscured in *Mardi*, which is one of Melville's most pessimistic works. There Melville depicts a man raising himself by sheer will and determination and stubborn but courageous blindness to a level almost of the unknowable forces that rule life and death and conspire to keep him down. But Taji's greatness is blurred by other characters and by a maze of philosophical discourse, especially on the futility of life; consequently the tragic effects of pity and fear, of admiration and horror, which Ahab draws forth, are only faintly felt by the reader of *Mardi*. It is, nevertheless, the richest and most complex of Melville's early novels.

THE NATURE OF EXPERIENCE:
The Howling Infinite

Part I

Chapter 2

Herman Melville's first book is a peculiar combination of autobiography, fiction, and borrowings. When viewed as a novel,
it may suddenly appear much like a travelogue. When approached
as autobiography, it seems starkly exaggerated and fictionalized.
When analyzed from the standpoint of its borrowings, it transcends them all, and the critic must face the question of why Melville borrowed what he did and why his own work is so much
greater than those books he borrowed from.

Typee was a fit work to inaugurate the career of Herman Melville, for it, like its author, defies classification. It has its own validity as a work of art, however, and like most of Melville's books
must be examined on its own terms. Always realizing that it is
based on Melville's own stay among the Typees in 1842 and that
he borrowed whole descriptions from such factual accounts of
Polynesian life as Charles S. Stewart's *A Visit to the South Seas
. . .* , Captain David Porter's *Journal of a Cruise Made to the
Pacific Ocean*, and William Ellis's *Polynesian Researches*, I intend
to treat *Typee* chiefly as a work of fiction. For whatever else it

9

might be, it is an artistic creation portraying in a narrative the inner life of a hero named Tommo, who may be Herman Melville, but if so only in a recreated and synthesized form such as that which the author of a novel so often takes when he pours himself into his hero.[1]

Tommo's journey into and out of Typee valley may have roughly paralleled Melville's own, but as D. H. Lawrence recognized a long time ago, it is also a symbolic journey which suggests the nature of experience. Lawrence's essay on *Typee*, to which many later analyses owe a great debt, discusses the book in terms of man's futile attempt to return to Eden after he has been scarred and deepened by centuries of collective experience.[2] Though man longs to go back to primitive innocence, he cannot fit in there and he must live in his own time and place. Most modern critics have followed Lawrence's lead in thinking of Typee as Eden or Innocence. F. O. Matthiessen, for example, wrote that Typee represents "a primitive state of innocence in which developing mankind may not remain. . . ."[3] Ronald Mason argued that "the key to the purpose of the book is the innocence of the Typees."[4] William Ellery Sedgwick expressed his view of Typee eloquently as a moment in time we all remember, a time of "spontaneous, instinctive being, in which human consciousness is a simple and happy undertaking of rudimentary sensations and simple sensuous im-

1. Leslie A. Fiedler, in *Love and Death in the American Novel* (New York, 1960), observes that Melville relived his early adventures imaginatively before he wrote of them: "Melville could not, it should be observed, have written in *Typee* and *Omoo* the simple truth, even if he had wanted to; for he was blessed with a notably poor memory and a rich imagination, which he bolstered with observations and data on the places he had been, drawn from other men's accounts. Though his first two books are written in the first person, their 'I' is not his old self who had lived among the cannibals, but an invention of the new self that had developed after his twenty-fifth year—before which, he tells us himself, he had no intellectual development" (pp. 521–22).

2. *Studies in Classic American Literature* (New York, 1923), pp. 193–207.

3. *American Renaissance* (New York, 1941), p. 288.

4. *The Spirit Above the Dust* (London, 1951), p. 26.

pressions; in which physical health and good animal spirits have a large preponderance; in which the impulses and affections of the human heart suffer no disguise nor any distortion; the phase, finally, in which as yet no painful cleavage is felt dividing a happy animality from the gentlest and most guileless impulses of the heart."[5]

Simple, innocent, Edenic—this is unquestionably one side of Typee as it is presented in the book. James E. Miller, Jr., rightly observes, however, that "this Polynesian retreat, though a Paradise in many respects and particularly to one weary of the outrageous behavior of civilization, still falls short of the original Garden." Indeed, there is "Horror that exists not far beneath the placid surface."[6] Just what this horror is has nowhere been better stated than by Sophia Hawthorne; in a letter to her mother she commented on "all this golden splendor and enchantment glowing before the dark refrain constantly brought as a background—the fear of being killed and eaten—the cannibalism in the olive tinted Apollos around him—the unfathomable mystery of their treatment of him."[7]

As Mrs. Hawthorne seemed to discern, there are two Typees, the one evoking joy and glad animal spirits, the other fear and horror. We are aware of the beautiful green valley, but also the harsh mountains that surround it; the beauty of the people, but also their unfathomable practice of tattooing; the delightful absence of civilized dogma, but also the countless and seemingly senseless taboos; the inherent good nature of the Typees, but their unpredictability and that unfortunate ritual of eating their enemies. Why, then, is *Typee* so frequently considered a sort of idyl of the South Seas? Charles R. Anderson, for example, has written that "*Typee* . . . is a wholehearted defense of the noble Savage and a

5. *Herman Melville: The Tragedy of Mind* (Cambridge, Mass., 1944), p. 28.

6. *A Reader's Guide to Herman Melville* (New York, 1962), pp. 30, 33.

7. Eleanor M. Metcalf, *Herman Melville: Cycle and Epicycle* (Cambridge, Mass., 1953), p. 91.

eulogy of his happy life, his external beauty, and his inner purity of heart. Virtually the whole book is written in the romantic literary tradition inaugurated by Rousseau a century before."[8] Such a view does not separate the two viewpoints of the book's narrator.[9] The purpose and complexity of the book unfold in the two separate perspectives, and the picture of Tommo, Melville's first hero, comes into focus.

In the Preface to *Typee* the reader is in the opening sentence

8. *Melville in the South Seas* (New York, 1939), p. 178. Geoffrey Stone, in *Melville* (New York, 1949), remarks that "by any strict literary criterion" *Typee* is no more than merely "a lively and pleasant book" (p. 56).

9. Of the dozens of critics who have analyzed *Typee* only a very few have seen the two levels of narration. Sedgwick makes the point briefly but does not develop it: "There is the perspective of the story proper, of the events at the time they happened; and there is the broader perspective of the book as a whole, in which the events of the story and their circumstances are seen at a distance of four years across all the light and shadow of Melville's experience in the interim" (p. 24).

A few of the points made in this chapter, including the distinction between Tommo of the past and the narrator Tommo, are also discussed in Edgar A. Dryden's provocative book, *Melville's Thematics of Form* (Baltimore, 1968), which appeared after my own chapter on *Typee* had been written. One of the major differences in our analyses is that Dryden portrays the older Tommo as much more mature (or initiated) than he is in my view. See pp. 33–46.

See also Newton Arvin, *Herman Melville* (New York, 1950), who comments on Tommo's "heightened 'anxiety' on the one hand, and a deliberate idyllism, on the other" (p. 83). Near the end of his chapter on *Typee*, Lawrance Thompson, in *Melville's Quarrel with God* (Princeton, 1952), makes this perceptive statement: "If Melville fought so hard to get away from that Earthly Paradise, how could he ever have idealized it? The answer is fairly easy: the Typee valley became Paradise for him only after he had left it, only after it had again become remote. Then he could look back at it wistfully, and glorify it as a symbol of something highly desirable but unobtainable, remote in both the past and the future: Paradise. While sampling this ultimate serenity, Melville had suffered egregiously and had longed to escape. But as soon as he had gotten far enough away from it, he suffered egregiously to think that there was no other place on earth quite like it" (p. 53). Sedgwick, Arvin, and Thompson, all suggest the dual perspective without developing the idea. Thus their treatments of *Typee* do not parallel mine.

made aware that a period of time has elapsed since Tommo experienced the adventures he is relating: "More than three years have elapsed since the occurrence of the events recorded in this volume. The interval, with the exception of the last few months, has been chiefly spent by the author tossing about on the wide ocean" (p. xiii). The significance of this remark goes far beyond a leisurely introduction to the narrator. It establishes the two points in time from which the experience is to be regarded—Tommo at the time of his stay with the Typees and Tommo after his escape and subsequent wanderings over the sea of life. In several other places the time lapse is underscored. In the first chapter the narrator recounts a humorous episode involving the native queen of Nukuheva "between two and three years after the adventures recorded in this volume" (p. 7). Several pages later he declares: "I may here state, and on my faith as an honest man, that though more than three years have elapsed since I left this same identical vessel [the *Dolly*], she still continues in the Pacific . . ." (p. 23). The functioning of this dual time scheme is suggested by such sentences as the following, in which the narrator presents first his puzzled state of mind over the Typees' behavior and then indicates that he has since answered the question: "Their singular behavior almost led me to imagine that they never before had beheld a white man; but a few moments' reflection convinced me that this could not have been the case; and a more satisfactory reason for their conduct has since suggested itself to my mind" (p. 74).

And so the narrative goes: part of it recounting Tommo's adventures and his feelings at that time and part of it commenting on the past from the vantage point of the present. The difference that such a distinction can make is readily apparent in a consideration of Tommo's state of mind while he lived in Typee. Without distinguishing between Tommo's reconstruction of his past and his retrospective comment, it might seem that Tommo had some rough moments among the Typees and that he doubtlessly wanted to leave them, but that overall he enjoyed himself aplenty. This viewpoint is expressed, for example, on the cover of a recent paperback edition of *Typee* (Doubleday's Dolphin series): "Although his final escape was treacherous, Melville enjoyed his merry, idle days in captivity among the cannibals, where, he reported later in *Typee*, he wooed a maiden and participated in such festivities as the Feast of the Calabashes." Actually, Tommo enjoyed himself precious little.

When Tommo and his companion Toby arrive in the valley of Typee, Tommo is extremely fearful, and the question "Happar or Typee?" occurs to him repeatedly. He has heard tales of the Typees' ferocity, and he worries that he and Toby might have stumbled into the Typees' dread valley—as indeed they have—instead of having reached the friendly Happars as they had hoped. "I remained distressingly alive to all the fearful circumstances of our present situation," he writes. "Was it possible that, after all our vicissitudes, we were really in the terrible valley of Typee, and at the mercy of its inmates, a fierce and unrelenting tribe of savages?" (p. 76). The painful uncertainty reflected in this passage prefigures Tommo's dominant state of mind while he is in Typee. The information and misinformation which he receives about the Typees before he reaches their valley serve two functions. They set up a dramatic contrast between what Tommo expected and what he actually finds. The Typees are not half so fierce as he had heard. On the other hand, Tommo's early expectations and opinion of the Typees suggest a preconditioning of mind which he never completely overcomes. Much of his later anxiety can be accounted for in terms of this preconditioning. It is thus easier to perceive and understand Tommo's frequent state of fear while he is among the Typees if we recall with what terror he thought of them before he ever saw them.

After a week among the Typees, Tommo is still "fairly puzzled," but he begins to feel that "the horrible character imputed to these Typees appeared ... wholly undeserved" (p. 97). Nevertheless he still has great apprehensions, and he quickly adds: "Notwithstanding the kind treatment we received, I was too familiar with the fickle disposition of savages not to feel anxious to withdraw from the valley, and put myself beyond the reach of that fearful death which, under all these smiling appearances, might yet menace us" (p. 97). He cannot think of escaping yet, however, because of some mysterious disease that has attacked his leg and made him lame. When Toby leaves the first time, Tommo becomes deeply depressed. Toby is injured by the Happars and brought back unconscious. "This incident," Tommo remarks, "threw a dark cloud over our prospects" (p. 102). They now realize, despondently, that there is little hope of escape. Tommo's spirits sink; his leg grows worse; and as he worries that "ere long we might be exposed to some caprice on the part of the islanders, I now gave up all hopes of recovery, and became a prey to the most gloomy thoughts. A deep dejection fell upon me . . ." (p. 104). Then Toby disappears, and with that, Tommo says, "hope deserted me, and I fell a victim to despair" (p. 109). He feels "bitter remorse" at having come to Typee and suspects that "these treacherous savages" had "made away" with Toby. "The conduct of the islanders appeared inexplicable" (p. 109).

Only for brief moments can Tommo forget his troubles, as in the evening when the native girls anoint his body with "aka." But even "in the midst of so many consolatory circumstances," Tommo was "consumed by the most dismal forebodings" and he "remained a prey to the profoundest melancholy" (p. 118). Meanwhile his leg continued to ache and "threatened the most fatal results." Probably the word used most to describe Tommo's feelings during his stay among the Typees is "despair." He feels it frequently when he realizes that he cannot escape: "Sick at heart, I reseated myself upon the mats, and for the moment abandoned myself to despair" (p. 120).

As if to retain his sanity, Tommo develops a form of insensibility; then his leg improves: "Gradually I lost all knowledge of the regular recurrence of the days of the week, and sunk insensibly into that kind of apathy which ensues after some violent outbreak of despair. My limb suddenly healed, the swelling went down, the pain subsided, and I had every reason to suppose that I should

15

soon completely recover from the affliction that had so long tor-
mented me" (p. 123). Then comes the only time during his stay
when he can truly enjoy himself. "Returning health and peace of
mind," he writes, "gave a new interest to everything around me.
I sought to diversify my time by as many enjoyments as lay within
reach" (p. 131). His constant aide and companion, Kory-Kory,
carries him daily to a small lake and watches over him while he
swims and romps with the native girls. He even manages to have
a rigid taboo eased so that "the beauteous Fayaway" can paddle
with him in his canoe.

His enjoyment is short-lived, however, for with the appearance
and departure of Marnoo a few pages later, all his anxieties about
Toby's fate and all "the most dreadful forebodings" return (p.
141). A "bitter pang" shoots through him as he realizes anew that
he is being kept prisoner. When Marnoo leaves, Tommo gives
himself "up to the most desponding reflections" (p. 142). Fearing
that the Typees may be aware of his great desire to escape, he
determines "to make the best of a bad bargain, and to bear up
manfully against whatever might betide" (p. 144). To allay their
suspicions, he tries to "bury all regrets, and all remembrances" of
his past life and fling himself "anew into all the social pleasures of
the valley . . ." (p. 144).

This mood is broken when he becomes deeply depressed over
the prospects of being tattooed: "From the time of my casual encounter with Karky the artist, my life was one of absolute wretch-
edness" (p. 231). Then the mysterious disease of his leg returns
with violence. His imagination runs wild after he sees evidence
of cannibalism, and he has "horrible apprehensions" about being
eaten: "My imagination ran riot in these horrid speculations, and
I felt certain that the worst possible evils would befal me" (p. 233).
After Marnoo's second visit, Tommo writes, "I was reduced to
such a state, that it was with extreme difficulty I could walk . . ."
(p. 243). These were days, like most of his days in Typee, "of suffering and sorrow" (p. 243). Shortly thereafter he escapes, "but

to such a state was I reduced," he says, "that three months elapsed before I recovered my health" (p. 253).

Such was Tommo's paradise. The question remains: if he suffered so much, physically and mentally, why do so many readers of *Typee* come away with the impression of a South Seas idyl? It is chiefly Tommo's retrospective commentary which causes that impression. In the extended recapitulation I have given above, none of that commentary was included. Tommo had an experience which was essentially negative; when he looks back over it he sometimes tells it straight—as much as it is possible to do so—but he sometimes romanticizes it. In the nearly four years after escaping from Typee, Tommo has seen much of civilization, and he has decided that the Typees, in retrospect, were not so bad after all and that his life there was more interesting than it actually was.

Tommo's retrospective comment, which frequently intrudes upon his narrative of despair, is marked by four moods. The first is nostalgia, which colors much of what he says as he remembers his stay in Typee. Tommo clearly yearns for the good old days.[10] "In looking back to this period," he says, "and calling to remembrance the numberless proofs of kindness and respect which I received from the natives of the valley," he finds it hard to understand why he was so miserable (p. 118). In the distance now, Typee seems almost like an Eden to him. Whenever passages such as the following appear in *Typee*, they suggest a mood developed over the years rather than a reflection of what Tommo felt while he lived with the natives: "The penalty of the Fall presses very lightly upon the valley of Typee. . . . Nature has planted the bread-fruit and the banana, and in her own good time she brings them to maturity, when the idle savage stretches forth his hand, and satisfies his appetite" (p. 195). Or "There were none of those thousand sources of irritation that the ingenuity of civilized man has created to mar

10. Lawrence makes this point with his usual intensity: "The past. The Golden Age of the past. What a nostalgia we all feel for it. Yet we won't want it when we get it. Try the South Seas" (p. 206).

his own felicity. There were no foreclosures of mortgages, no protested notes, no bills payable, no debts of honor in Typee; no unreasonable tailors and shoemakers, perversely bent on being paid; . . . no destitute widows with their children starving on cold charities of the world; no beggars; no debtors' prisons" (p. 126).

Tommo makes it clear that the more he travels the world and the more he sees of humankind, the more Typee seems in retrospect an Eden. In Typee he began to have a rather high estimate of human nature, "but alas! since then I have been one of the crew of a man-of-war, and the pent-up wickedness of five hundred men has nearly overturned all my previous theories" (p. 203). His changing opinion could be charted perhaps in these terms: he originally maintained a very low opinion of the Typees, so low in fact that when he actually lived among them he found them strikingly unlike what he had expected, but when he left them and saw more of the world—then, they seemed positively noble by comparison. They have come to represent to him the Noble Savage, and nostalgically he looks back and praises their beauty of form and spirit, forgetting from time to time how he hated Typee when he was there. "All hail, therefore, Mehevi, King of the Cannibal Valley," he cries, "and long life and prosperity to his Typeean Majesty! May Heaven for many a year preserve him . . ." (p. 189).

When the nostalgic mood is upon him, Tommo can even excuse the Typees for the aberration that horrified him most: "The reader will ere long have reason to suspect that the Typees are not free from the guilt of cannibalism; and he will then, perhaps, charge me with admiring a people against whom so odious a crime is chargeable. But this only enormity in their character is not half so horrible as it is usually described" (p. 205).

Nostalgia in its purest form is reflected when Tommo sighs: "In the valley of Typee ice-creams would never be rendered less acceptable by sudden frosts, nor would picnic parties be deferred on account of inauspicious snowstorms: for there day follows day in one unvarying round of summer and sunshine, and the whole year is one long tropical month of June just melting into July" (p. 213).

Where has the rain gone? In that tortuous journey he and Toby make through the mountains, rain falls frequently, but from the moment they reach Typee valley, rain is mentioned but once—and that time in a general comment on how showers in Typee are "intermitting and refreshing." Unless the Typees are suffering one of their rare droughts—and there is no evidence that they are—rain must have fallen during the four months Tommo lived with them.[11] The fact that he remembers the valley as a place of constant and unvarying sunshine is further evidence of the nostalgia that sometimes distorts his retrospective vision.

Nostalgia is an emotion closely related to homesickness, and there is considerable evidence that Tommo has come to think of Typee with that feeling. Typee is in a sense a kind of home to him. From the first he thinks of Tinor and old Marheyo kindly as parental figures. He is made a part of the household, and Kory-Kory is as faithful as any brother could be. Fayaway may be more a sister than a mistress. Tommo's escape in the final chapter resembles running away from home rather than running to home. He is surrounded by his Typeean family. Together they make up a kind of domestic tableau: "Every one had left me except Marheyo, Kory-Kory, and poor dear Fayaway, who clung to me, sobbing indignantly" (p. 250). They know that he wishes to leave them, but they do not understand the reason. Although it pains him, old Marheyo allows his wayward "son" to leave home. In the climactic moment of the final chapter Marheyo aids Tommo in his escape: "In the midst of this tumult old Marheyo came to my side, and I shall never forget the benevolent expression of his countenance. He placed his arm upon my shoulder, and emphatically pronounced the only two English words I had taught him—'home' and 'mother.' I at once understood what he meant, and eagerly expressed my thanks to him" (p. 248).

It is not at all clear that Tommo actually understood Marheyo

11. Melville's own stay with the Typees was probably much shorter than Tommo's. He was there a few weeks at most. Anderson estimates it at slightly over four weeks (p. 192).

any better here than he had throughout his stay with him. The old man is even more inexplicable than the other natives. Tommo observes with wonder and incomprehension as Marheyo constructs a house that never seems to get built, sits for hours perched in a tree top, bathes at extremely odd times in a stream, or stalks through the brush with Tommo's old shoes proudly dangling from his neck. At the time of his escape Tommo thought Marheyo was telling him that he understood—that he knew Tommo wanted to return to his home and mother and that he would help him. But it seems just as likely that old Marheyo was expressing his own affection for Tommo and was trying to let him know that his home and mother were here, in Typee, and that he considered him a member of his family. Since Tommo seemed determined to run away, however, old Marheyo unselfishly helped him in whatever way he could. Tommo could not at that time have considered Typee his real home, but as he views the whole experience in retrospect, he often seems to be feeling something akin to homesickness, and ironically old Marheyo's words take on new meaning.

Tommo's second mood as he looks back is righteous anger, which characterizes that body of commentary charging various evils against civilization and voicing Tommo's thorough disapproval of missionaries. "Ill-fated people!" he cries. "I shudder when I think of the change a few years will produce in their paradisaical abode; and probably when most destructive vices, and the worst attendances on civilization, shall have driven all peace and happiness from the valley, the magnanimous French will proclaim to the world that the Marquesas Islands have been converted to Christianity! and this the Catholic world will doubtless consider as a glorious event. Heaven help the 'Isles of the Sea!'" (p. 195). Such preachments against the civilized world are digressions and represent the feelings of the narrator in the *present*, not his feelings or opinions while he lived with the Typees.

Tommo's anger toward the missionaries is also a reflection of his present state of mind. He apparently knew little about the work of missionaries in the South Seas until after his experience in

Typee. He admits, "Not until I visited Honolulu [after Typee] was I aware of the fact that the small remnant of the natives had been civilized into draft horses, and evangelized into beasts of burden. But so it is. They have been literally broken into the traces, and are harnessed to the vehicles of their spiritual instructors like so many dumb brutes!" (p. 196). Thus, having lived among the Typees and then in subsequent years heard of and seen first-hand the bumbling and sometimes destructive efforts of missionaries, the narrator interrupts his reconstruction of the past to voice his present indignation at the lack of understanding manifested in missionary work among the natives. Tommo's sermonizing about the wrongs of the civilized world and the narrowness of missionaries produces the general impression of a broad-minded man living among a primitive people and appreciating as most men could not the simplicity and genuineness he finds there. As we have seen, this was far from the case.

The third mood in Tommo's retrospective narrative helps a great deal to blunt the keen sense of past recurrent suffering. It is the comfortable objectivity of the various and often extended descriptions of practically every phase of Typeean life. While Tommo is living among the Typees, he notices much but understands very little. He finds the natives unfathomable and their ways inexplicable. He is always trying to get answers to his questions, to "find out," as he puts it, "the meaning of the strange things that were going on" (p. 168). His failure to understand what he sees accounts for much of his frustration and agony. "I saw everything," he says, "but could comprehend nothing" (p. 177). All is a mystery to him. Yet it sometimes appears that he observed and understood very well, for parts of the book make up an excellent travelogue. Here is a man who in recounting his terribly depressing stay among cannibals frequently interrupts his narrative of despair to assume the stance of a tourist and to tell in a relaxed voice and in detail all about the breadfruit tree and the making of tapa. He describes a typical day in Typee valley, the ancient stone terraces, the Feast of the Calabashes, the preparation of arva, the cooking of hogs, a chief's tomb, the Typees' religious practices, the various civil institutions of Typee, matrimonial relationships among the natives, burial procedures, and a Typeean fishing party. Finally he recounts the natural history of the valley, which includes comments on dogs, cats, and various other matters. How could a traveler who noted all that so thoroughly have time to be miserable?

Again, these descriptions come from the narrator's present state of mind. They grow out of years of looking back on and reflecting and reading about the things he saw in Typee. And since there are so many of them and since they interrupt the main narrative so often, they have the effect of making his suffering seem less prolonged and intense. For example, after describing how he felt when Marnoo leaves, Tommo waits twelve chapters before telling us again what he was thinking and how he felt. During those eighty pages he tells of a few things that happened in the valley, but he spends most of the time in describing Typee and its customs.

A fourth mood is seen in the light commentary, which is often humorous. One of the most amusing episodes in the book involves Tommo's bad leg. When Mehevi first sees the situation he immediately calls for "an aged islander, who might have been taken for old Hippocrates himself" (p. 79). The old fellow is not as gentle as he looks, however, for he at once sets to work pinching and hammering Tommo's painfully sensitive leg with absolute vigor: "He fastened on the unfortunate limb as if it were something for which he had been long seeking, and muttering some kind of incantation continued his discipline, pounding it after a fashion that set me well nigh crazy" (p. 80). While this is going on, Toby frantically gestures, trying to stop Tommo's "tormentor": "To have looked at my companion . . . one would have thought that he was the deaf and dumb alphabet incarnated" (p. 80). When this strange form of treatment does finally end, Tommo's leg is "left much in the same condition as a rump-steak after undergoing the castigating process which precedes cooking" (p. 80). Now this episode is more comic than serious because of the way Tommo describes it as he views it through the film of years. It certainly was not at all amusing when it happened.

The effect produced by such incidents as the Typeean doctor's treatment of Tommo's afflicted leg is something like that which results when one listens to a talented story-teller relating with a grin anecdotes about his adventurous past. The listener may get the erroneous impression that the narrator always enjoyed himself tremendously because of his present amusement. There were moments when Tommo was mildly amused and entertained by what he saw, but the amusement and entertainment are magnified many times through the passage of years. For example, in one of those rare periods when he is able to appreciate the Typees' sheer love of life, Tommo makes a pop-gun for a child from a piece of bamboo. It causes a sensation, and Typees of all ages line up to have Tommo produce one of the marvelous toys for them. For several days sounds of the pop-guns are heard throughout the valley. Any slight annoyance that Tommo might once have felt in having to make so many toys—he finally manages to train an assistant in their manufacture—and any other disagreeable aspects of the pop-gun incident are completely lost as he reminisces about it in the most bemused terms of mock-heroism: "Pop, Pop, Pop, Pop, now resounded all over the valley. Duels, skirmishes, pitched battles, and general engagements were to be seen on every side. Here, as you walked along a path which led through a thicket, you fell into a cunningly-laid ambush, and became a target for a body of musketeers whose tattooed limbs you could just see peeping into view through the foliage. There, you were assailed by the intrepid garrison of a house, who levelled their bamboo rifles at you from between the upright canes which composed its sides. Farther on you were fired upon by a detachment of sharpshooters, mounted upon the top of a pi-pi" (p. 145).

Tommo therefore narrates from two perspectives—then and now. His present moods—nostalgia, anger, objective observance, and humor—frequently intrude upon the narrative which describes his actual states of mind while he was in Typee. The result shows clearly two views of Typee and emphasizes the changing subjective quality of that entire experience for Tommo.

In a larger framework the two views of Typee suggest a fundamental concept of reality—namely, that it is ultimately unknowable. One of the most important questions to be raised after perceiving Tommo's double perspective is this: which of his views of Typee is the right one? Or, indeed, is it possible to have a true view of Typee? The past seems to become confused with the present. An experience such as Tommo's is complex and organic and does not end abruptly but undergoes transformation as it continues to be a part of his mind. The pure past, then, is irrecoverable. That warning resounds throughout *Typee*, which is very much a book about the past.

Tommo finds that lesson difficult to learn. He is the first hero Melville created and quite possibly the most naive, for he never seems to grasp the nature of the past or to realize that he cannot go back. His journey to Typee is both real and symbolic. Lawrence argued that it suggests an attempted return to the past of the race: "The heart of the Pacific is still the Stone Age; in spite of steamers. The heart of the Pacific seems like a vast vacuum in which, miragelike, continues the life of myriads of ages back."[12] Lawrence's argument is based on his view of Typee as a primitive Eden, which is no longer possible for modern man. The point is perceptive and interesting, but what Tommo is searching for can also be expressed in more personal and less mythic terms. If, as Lawrence states, Tommo wants to go back, it is his own past he yearns for, perhaps the joyous time of childhood. What I want to suggest here, therefore, is that Tommo's desire to leave his ship for something better is a longing for some past happy state in his experience, which he contrasts to his present restlessness.

Tommo seems to be yearning for past happier times when near the beginning he makes it clear that he cannot live in the present

12. *Studies in Classic American Literature*, p. 196.

situation and can see no relief in the future. He feels surrounded by a crew "composed of a parcel of dastardly and mean-spirited wretches . . ." (p. 21). Knowing how long whaling voyages can last, he concludes that "there was little to encourage one in looking forward to the future, especially as I had always had a presentiment that we should make an unfortunate voyage, and our experience so far had justified the expectation" (p. 23). His original plan of escape does not involve Typee or even the friendly Happar Valley. He merely wants to hide out in what he believes to be the lovely mountains that look down on the bay and to watch from that point ("with a cluster of plantains within easy reach") until his ship leaves. Then he plans to come down to Nukuheva and to make an "agreeable" visit with the friendly natives until a good opportunity for leaving the island presents itself.

It is a childish plan. Yet it might be expected of the Tommo who tells us early in the book that "I had made up my mind to 'run away' " (p. 20). He has sailed on a ship called *Dolly*, a name that suggests the world of childhood. What he finds on board the *Dolly*, however, is opposite from the joy and innocence of childhood. The world of the *Dolly* is quite distinctly adult, with all its imperfection, and Tommo finds it intolerable. What he wants is a situation that is congenial to his own youth and naiveté. He cannot find it on the *Dolly*. He feels imprisoned and decides to run away.

Thus the basic structural pattern of the book is established—escape and return. In the beginning Tommo is depicted as a young man who cannot accept the sordidness and uncertainties of the world; he is, in a sense, a child among adults. Isolated and unhappy, he would like nothing better than to go back into a time in his life when cruelty and selfishness and unhappiness were relatively unknown. In *Typee* he symbolically goes back. There he finds a situation closely resembling childhood.[13] After his first

13. Miller comments that "like children or animals, their [the Typees'] affection and sweetness can be instantly converted to hate and treachery. That same instinct and spontaneity which make them so charming and attractive can also render them repulsive and horrible" (pp. 33–34). See also Richard

night in the valley, he awakes and sees around him "faces in which childish delight and curiosity were vividly portrayed" (p. 77). As he lives among the Typees, they seem more and more like children. Even in battles with their enemies they run about making sounds that resemble "the halloos of a parcel of truant boys who had lost themselves in the woods" (p. 129). They seem scarcely more serious or mature in their profoundest religious affairs, for "in the celebration of many of their strange rites, they appeared merely to seek a sort of childish amusement" (p. 174). The chief idol is like a "doll" which the priest Kolory "alternately fondles and chides" (p. 176), and "the whole of these proceedings were like those of a parcel of children playing with dolls and baby houses" (p. 176).[14] What little work or food gathering they do reminds Tommo of children at play. Narnee, a young chief, starts up a tree to gather coconuts, and "as if defeated in this childish attempt, he now sinks to the earth despondingly, beating his breast in well-acted despair; and then, starting to his feet all at once, and throwing back his head, raises both hands, like a school-boy about to catch a falling ball" (p. 214). After that exhibition he goes on to climb the tree and fling the nuts to the ground.

In every area of life the Typees are described in terms of childhood. Tommo was unhappy in the adult world, and he escaped to a child's world. But he is even more unhappy there. Once growing out of childhood, he cannot again be a part of it. In Typee his situation is reversed from that on board the *Dolly*. He is now an adult among children. The anxiety and despair which he experi-

---

Chase, *Herman Melville* (New York, 1949), who argues that Tommo's being fed poi by Kory-Kory is symbolic: "For the hero, with a sad gaiety, was reliving his childhood in terms of the entrancingly fitting symbolic objects of which Typee Valley so expertly consisted" (p. 11). Chase's interpretation is largely Freudian. He sees Tommo attempting to "withdraw into the recesses of his own infantile sexuality."

14. One of Melville's sources, Captain David Porter's *Journal of a Cruise Made to the Pacific Ocean*, contains the following observation: "In religion these people are mere children; their morals are their baby-houses, and their gods are their dolls." Quoted in Anderson, p. 173.

ences in Typee define what it means to be an adult in a child's world: he is completely alienated. He cannot communicate with the children. Their ways and their thinking are inexplicable to him, and he lives in fear because they are as unpredictable as children. All men yearn at times to return to the sunshine of childhood. In *Typee* Melville portrayed a man who got his wish. And that man could not wait to escape and return to the adult world.

If he felt imprisoned on the *Dolly*, he is many times more aware of being "hemmed in" with the Typees. Frequently Melville uses imagery that suggests Tommo's captive situation. Typee valley is hemmed in by the forbidding mountains that Tommo painfully passed through to get there. He is aware that he is also "hemmed in by hostile tribes" (p. 102), and cannot pass through their lands. The Typees will not even consider letting him go. He is their captive plaything. They are as mysterious to him as the mind of a child is to an adult. His opportunity for running away comes just before he is physically and psychologically destroyed by a strange and beautiful world of childlike natives.

Tommo's return to the adult world, however, does not bring him peace. After months of recovering and then years of traveling about, he once again feels hemmed in. He suffers from the absurdities of civilized dogmas which press in on him. He is surrounded by human beings who are so lacking in dignity and decency that his estimate of human nature falls considerably. After nearly four years he has to run away again. He has experienced a great deal, but maturity has not come with it. He thinks he can return to the past again, this time by recapturing it in his imagination, by calling up Typee. He sits down to write a narrative, and the reader sees what Tommo cannot—that he is the sum total of all his experience, including those years of wandering *after* he left Typee, and that he can never go back, can never remember it as it actually was, because of what he has since become. While he was on the *Dolly*, he dreamed of an Elysium of childhood; finding that Typee was not Elysium, he returned, but he was not back long before the naive dream began anew.

Separating each escape and return is a trial, a painful experience which tests the mettle of the hero and acts as a barrier preventing his returning the same way as he escaped. When Tommo and Toby run away from the *Dolly*, they must make their way through hazardous chasms and steep mountains with little food. It is almost as if they have entered a damp inferno:

Five foaming streams, rushing through as many gorges, and swelled and turbid by the recent rains, united together in one mad plunge of nearly eighty feet, and fell with wild uproar into a deep black pool scooped out of the gloomy-looking rocks that lay piled around, and thence in one collected body dashed down a narrow sloping channel which seemed to penetrate into the very bowels of the earth. Overhead, vast roots of trees hung down from the sides of the ravine dripping with moisture, and trembling with the concussions produced by the fall. It was now sunset, and the feeble uncertain light that found its way into these caverns and woody depths heightened their strange appearance, and reminded us that in a short time we should find ourselves in utter darkness. (p. 45)

Here Tommo and Toby spend the first terrible night of their journey. "The accumulated horrors of that night," he says, "the deathlike coldness of the place, the apalling darkness and the dismal sense of our forlorn condition, almost unmanned me" (p. 46). They spend five nights chilled and wet. Tommo's injured leg and the accompanying fever nearly drive him out of his mind. During the day they alternately climb steep inclines and make their way down cavernous ravines, wandering without direction, until they finally chance upon Typee.

Although the mountain journey is the most extensively detailed trial in the book, two other experiences occur that must be surmounted before Tommo can make his escapes. To reach civilization again, he must kill a man, the fierce Mow-Mow. After pushing off from the land, Tommo and his rescuers encounter a group of the natives attempting to cut off their escape. As Mow-Mow swims toward the boat, Tommo painfully realizes what he must do:

"Even at the moment I felt horror at the act I was about to commit; but it was no time for pity or compunction, and with a true aim, and exerting all my strength, I dashed the boat-hook at him. It struck him just below the throat, and forced him downwards. I had no time to repeat my blow, but I saw him rise to the surface in the wake of the boat, and never shall I forget the ferocious expression of his countenance" (p. 252). Tommo's other trial is only casually mentioned, but it is of great importance. After escaping Typee and living once again among civilized people, he has recently "been one of the crew of a man-of-war," he says, and that was an experience in unqualified and undiluted evil, a nightmare of concentrated wickedness. He had to go through this trial of a floating hell as a psychological preparation for writing down much of what is in *Typee*. Had he not undergone the man-of-war experience, Typee might not have looked so fine to him in retrospect and he might not have revisited it imaginatively.

These hellish experiences, which are necessary for all three escapes—the first to Typee, the second away from Typee, and third to Typee again (but this time in the imagination), act as barriers to Tommo's returning over the same route. After those terrible days in the mountains he thinks it practically impossible to go back over them. After killing Mow-Mow he has cut himself off from Typee. He can never make another actual visit there on friendly terms. Nor does he have the stomach for returning to the real and imperfect world through sailing again aboard a man-of-war. Therefore, when he escapes from Typee, it is by way of the sea, not over the mountains; when he returns to Typee, it is not by really going there but by thinking and writing about it; and when he finishes his narrative and returns once again to the outside world, the imperfect adult world, it will doubtlessly be by a different means than a man-of-war. Even if the course first traveled were not so painful, however, Tommo would still find another route to try to return by, as he explains early in the book: "There is scarcely anything when a man is in difficulties that he is more disposed to look upon with abhorrence than a right-about retrograde movement—a systematic going over of the already trodden ground; and especially if he has a love of adventure, such a course appears indescribably repulsive, so long as there remains the least hope to be derived from braving untried difficulties" (p. 54).

Tommo's comment about "retrograde movement" is significantly revealing. He is Melville's hero not yet mature. As Newton Arvin perceptively put it: "Not in avoiding the clash between consciousness and the unconscious, between mind and emotion, between anxious doubt and confident belief, but in confronting these antinomies head-on and, hopefully, transcending them—in that direction, as Melville intuitively saw, lay his right future as an adult person."[15] Nevertheless, it is clear that Tommo has the makings of the kind of searching hero Melville later depicts with admiration. He is a man "in difficulties" with his surroundings as Melville's later heroes all are. He has not, however, learned enough yet about the complex and ambiguous nature of experience; his restlessness leads him backward instead of forward. Yet he knows the danger of "retrograde movement," and his backward searching is over untried routes. Like the rest of Melville's heroes he is no systematizer. He is young, but already he distrusts the dogmas and systems he sees mankind worshipping. Within him is that distinctive "love of adventure" which in a later hero develops into the preference of the "howling infinite" over the "lee shore." When Tommo realizes that there is no Typee left to him and that he must take his search to the open sea, he will then be an Ishmael.

15. *Herman Melville*, p. 88.

REDBURN: *The Apples of Sodom*

Chapter 3

Melville wrote *Redburn* while still smarting from the slaps of reviewers who had found his previous book, *Mardi*, wild and foolish. Some of them had gone so far as to advise him to give up the involved allegorical method of *Mardi* and go back to the pristine simplicity of *Typee* and *Omoo*. He was smarting, too, from increased financial pressures. Now when he really needed money to support a wife and child, his third book promised to bring him considerably less in royalties than his first two.

It is no wonder, then, that *Redburn* was not a labor of love.[1] After the cool reception given *Mardi*, Melville found that to be practical he had to do something he did not want to do—to start all over again, to write the kind of book that would appeal to the same readers who had enjoyed *Typee* so thoroughly. With almost gruesome determination he saw the task through.

---

1. Hershel Parker argues that when Melville began *Redburn* his attitude was one of resolution rather than bitterness. See the "Historical Note" to *Redburn*, Northwestern-Newberry Edition of *The Writings of Herman Melville* (Evanston and Chicago, 1969), IV, 318.

The book he wrote was a great deal better than he ever admitted, but his frame of mind at that time produced two important results. The first was haste of composition. He wrote steadily on *Redburn* from the late spring of 1849 through the early summer and completed it in the record time of less than ten weeks.[2] Once finished, he took almost no time for revisions, but sent the manuscript as it was to his publisher to be set in type immediately. Consequently several rough places are evident in the plot. Early in the story, for example, he describes a sailor, Max the Dutchman, as "an old bachelor" (p. 79), and several chapters later gives him not one wife but two! (p. 128). In another instance Redburn goes away from his first voyage having been cheated by Captain Riga out of all his wages. Where he gets the money for his passage home is never explained.[3] In addition Melville apparently forgot that Harry Bolton had already signed (in Redburn's presence) to ship on the *Highlander* when he has Redburn ask Harry what he plans to do upon returning from London.[4]

Lack of revision was also partly responsible for a problem in point of view.[5] As in all Melville's early works the point of view

2. Ibid., p. 315.

3. These two slips are pointed out by William H. Gilman in *Melville's Early Life and "Redburn"* (New York, 1951), p. 208.

4. Parker, p. 320.

5. In recent years point of view has been the central issue in critical discussions of Melville's art in *Redburn*. F. O. Matthiessen was probably the first to argue that the "center of consciousness" shifts in the book (*American Renaissance*, New York, 1941, p. 397). Gilman agrees, calling the shifting of narrative voice from boy to adult a "ruinous defect." In *Melville's Quarrel with God* (Princeton, 1952) Lawrance Thompson contended that there are three, not two, points of view—that of the young Redburn, that of the older Redburn, and that of Melville himself, who satirizes the other two. Merlin Bowen, in "*Redburn* and the Angle of Vision," *Modern Philology*, LII (1954), 100–109, denies that there is any other narrative voice except that of the older Redburn: "And as for any marked 'shift in the angle of vision,' one must simply deny that it ever actually takes place" (p. 102). For an excellent summary of the entire problem of point of view, see Parker, pp. 348–49. Parker makes an effort to reconcile the various views by suggesting that "Melville's tone is not consistently satirical toward either the younger or the

is no simple matter. In *Redburn* it is complicated by the fact that the protagonist is the youngest in Melville's early work and the narrator probably the oldest. The two are of course the same person, but in a sense quite different, as all older people are different from their younger selves. To add to the complexity, the young Redburn is depicted in the process of maturing, so that he cannot be precisely the same boy at the end of the voyage as he was before it. There have to be three Redburns in the story, therefore: the older narrator, the very naive boy, and the more experienced youngster at the end. There should be, however, only *one* narrative voice—that of the older Redburn looking back. Melville wanted to separate his narrator widely from the boy of the story;[6] so he created a tone of voice which is sometimes condescending, sometimes sympathetic, occasionally mocking, and generally characterized by what the narrator himself calls "comical sadness" as he looks back. This oxymoronic combination accurately describes the older Redburn's attitude toward his past. By separating the narrator from the protagonist and further distinguishing subtly between the protagonist as a green boy and then as a tempered and tested youth, Melville could show his hero in at least three different stages of life.

If Melville did not quite bring it off, it is because there are four rather than three Redburns in the book, this last one an intruder which careful revision would have disposed of. The unwanted Redburn is not heard, as some critics have insisted, in the narrative voice which describes and comments. There is, as Merlin Bowen has argued, only one such voice.[7] The unwanted Redburn, a

---

older Redburn and that the narrative voice is not consistently that of the older Redburn" (p. 349).

6. Chapter titles, among other things, suggest such a separation. The narrator mentions himself in over half the sixty-two chapter titles, but never once uses the pronoun "I." Generally "he" is used and sometimes "Redburn" ("He Arrives in Town"; "He Gets a Peep at Ireland . . ."; "What Redburn saw in Launcelott's-Hey").

7. *"Redburn* and the Angle of Vision," pp. 100–102.

gremlin who confuses the reader and tries to spoil Melville's art, slips into the *dialogue*, mostly in the latter part of the book. The Redburn who says to his friend Harry Bolton, "My dear Bury, I have no more voice for a ditty, than a dumb man has for an oration. Sing? Such Macadamized lungs have I, that I think myself well off, that I can talk; let alone nightingaling" (p. 280)—this Redburn is not the boy who has just got back from Liverpool. This is an older actor in the events of the story who should not be there. Several times he intrudes, enough to obscure slightly an otherwise skillful achievement in point of view.

Anxious to get the job done, Melville worked too hastily and thereby created problems in details of plot and in point of view. The second important result of his determination to abandon, at least temporarily, the kind of creative endeavor which *Mardi* represented was his return to the same subject which he had explored in *Typee*. His fourth book, therefore, is actually more closely related in theme to his first than to any other of his novels.

The major theme of *Redburn* is succinctly expressed in a passage from *Typee*. Lost in the mountains around Nukuheva, Toby and Tommo (who is burning with fever) come upon a stream:

> In a few minutes we reached the foot of the gorge, and kneeling upon a small ledge of dripping rocks, I bent over to the stream. What a delicious sensation was I now to experience! I paused for a second to concentrate all my capabilities of enjoyment, and then immerged my lips in the clear element before me. Had the apples of Sodom turned to ashes in my mouth, I could not have felt a more startling revulsion. A single drop of the cold fluid seemed to freeze every drop of blood in my body; the fever that had been burning in my veins gave place on the instant to death-like chills, which shook me one after another like so many shocks of electricity, while the perspiration produced by my late violent exertions congealed in icy beads upon my forehead. My thirst was gone, and I fairly loathed the water. (p. 53)

The central situations in *Typee* and *Redburn* are essentially the same: a man burns with "fever," hungering and thirsting after something to alleviate the fever of his soul and satisfy his craving. Instead he finds ashes and the fever becomes chills. Like Tommo, Redburn immerged his "lips in the clear element" of experience, but what he tasted was bitter and unsatisfying. *Redburn* thus deals with the two aspects of this same idea: the fact of human hunger and the difference between expectation and experience.

Unsatisfied cravings in *Redburn* are projected through images of hunger. Young Wellingborough Redburn leaves his home and family because of a combination of his "naturally roving disposition"—a hunger to experience life—and "sad disappointments" in finances, which had left him and his family only one step from literal starvation (p. 3). As the narrator describes his early life, he seems almost preoccupied with eating or the desire to eat. He remembers being greatly impressed by a certain adventurer whom his aunt pointed out to him. " 'See what big eyes he has,' whispered my aunt, 'they got so big, because when he was almost dead with famishing in the desert, he all at once caught sight of a date tree, with the ripe fruit hanging on it' " (p. 5).[8]

The image of the date tree remains stamped upon Redburn's mind; it represents symbolically the goal of a youth who seeks "in a thousand ways," as he puts it, "to gratify my taste" (p. 6). An oil painting of his father's, a sea scene, appeals to his roving nature and, continuing the metaphor of hunger, he says: "I used to think a piece of it might taste good" (p. 6). Among his father's other possessions is "an old-fashioned glass ship, about eighteen inches long, and of French manufacture" (p. 7). This ship has entertained Melville's critics for a long time. Because it is glass and because it later is damaged, it has suggested to many Redburn's world of romantic illusion or innocence which is shattered upon his voyage to Liverpool.[9] Perhaps even more significant, however, is the fact

8. For a discussion of the possible identity of this adventurer, see Dorothee Metlitsky Finkelstein, *Melville's Orienda* (New Haven, 1961), pp. 51–52.

9. Ronald Mason, in *The Spirit Above the Dust* (London, 1951), connects the glass ship with the "romanticism of adolescence," and argues that it represents "the essence of the glamour of the sea" (p. 75).

that it brings out a certain hunger, a "temporary madness," in Redburn, for every time he sees it he hungrily wants to break into its tiny hull. He tells us that "I have always been in want, ever since I could remember" (p. 8), and he thinks that if he could just pry open the hull of the glass ship he might find there the wealth of Spanish gold coins that would help him to satisfy his deep hunger. The ship finally has to be placed on the mantel-piece to prevent Redburn from breaking into it.

If the boy Redburn had found the date tree, he might have discovered (as did Tommo at the stream) bitterness instead of nourishment and sweetness. If he had actually eaten the mellow old oil painting, he would have tasted only the stale canvas. If he had broken into the ship, he would have found no gold guineas but only shattered fragments of glass. These three symbols in Chapter 1—the date tree, the painting, and the glass ship—suggest that man's hunger can never be appeased.

As Redburn leaves home, the symbols of the soul's cravings are replaced by numerous references to actual food and hunger. On the boat which takes him down the Hudson River to New York, Redburn's isolation is depicted through his contrast with the well-fed passengers around him. They appear always to have just finished a sumptuous meal, while he has nothing to eat during the entire trip. After breakfast they nap on the settees or read; Redburn watches them from afar and worries because he does not have enough money for the fare. After dinner the other passengers, who are "waked up with their roast-beef and mutton," begin to chat, but the hungry Redburn has to remain isolated: "I sat apart, though among them" (p. 12). His isolation and hunger are intensified as he gazes at a "jovial party," eating and drinking: "Their faces were flushed with the good dinner they had eaten; and mine felt pale and wan with the long fast" (p. 12). When Redburn reaches New York and the home of his brother's friend, Mr. Jones, he is given a good meal, and for a time the world seems kind and his future promising.

Like most young men Redburn has at this point a profound

belief in the satisfactions of eating. "Every mouthful," he says of the first meal he has at Mr. Jones's house, "pushed the devil that had been tormenting me all day farther and farther out of me, till at last I entirely ejected him with three successive bowls of Bohea" (p. 15). The remedy for hunger, therefore, is food, a simple formula which Redburn carries over and tries to apply to every area of his craving. He had no real chance to find the date tree, to eat the oil painting, or to break into the glass ship; but he does have an opportunity to leave home in order to satisfy his hunger for experience. So he sets out with the same full faith that he has when he sits down hungrily at a meal. What he is to learn in the course of his initial voyage is that *meals*, literal and figurative, do not always satisfy.

The first painful experience that introduces Redburn to this truth comes after a prolonged period without food. Having thrown his last penny into the sea, he is unable to buy even a doughnut to eat before his ship gets underway. He has already told Mr. Jones goodbye, and thus would be embarrassed to return to him for another meal. Consequently he puts on a "bold look," drinks a big glass of water, and tries not to faint. "But this made me very qualmish," he says, "and soon I felt sick as death; my head was dizzy; and I went staggering along the walk, almost blind" (p. 26). With consternation he learns that he will receive no food until the ship leaves the dock. His period of hunger seems an eternity. Through several hours he suffers, relieving himself occasionally with water and a stolen carrot. The moment of departure finally arrives, and the word is passed for the crew to go to dinner. The order, Redburn says, "made my heart jump with delight, for now my long fast would be broken" (p. 31). Furthermore, he finds that he will have most of the food to himself because the newly arrived sailors are too full or too drunk to eat. His anticipated moment of ecstasy, however, is very much like Tommo's at the stream. "To my surprise," he writes, "I found that I could eat little or nothing; for now I only felt deadly faint, but not hungry" (p. 31). He finds himself in exactly the same situation as the speaker in a poem by

Emily Dickinson (who knew as well as anybody the phenomenon of the disappearing appetite). She "had been hungry, all the years," but when she could at last eat all she wanted,

> The Plenty hurt me—'twas so new—
> Myself felt ill—and odd—
> As Berry—of a Mountain Bush—
> Transplanted—to the Road—
>
> Nor was I hungry—so I found
> That Hunger—was a way
> Of Persons outside Windows—
> The Entering—takes away—[10]

It was perhaps a new experience to Redburn to be so hungry that he could not eat, but it was not the last time he would encounter the phenomenon. His own experience with severe hunger is merely the preparation for the most celebrated scene in the book—the appearance of the starving woman in Launcelott's-Hey. F. O. Matthiessen considered it the novel's "most unforgettable chapter."[11] Ronald Mason saw it as the episode where Redburn grows up.[12]

Redburn's outrage at the cruel indifference of society reaches its peak in this episode. He can find no one willing to help the starving woman and her children. They remain totally alone, their hunger unrecognized by others. "Ah! what are our creeds," he cries, "and how do we hope to be saved? Tell me, oh Bible, that story of Lazarus again, that I may find comfort in my heart for the poor and forlorn. Surrounded as we are by the wants and woes of our fellow-men, and yet given to follow our own pleasures, regardless of their pains, are we not like people sitting up with a corpse, and

10. *The Poems of Emily Dickinson*, ed. Thomas H. Johnson (Cambridge, Mass., 1955), II, 443.

11. *American Renaissance*, p. 397.

12. *The Spirit Above the Dust*, p. 75.

making merry in the house of the dead?" (p. 184). Frustrated in his attempts to get help for the family, Redburn can do no better than bring them a few scraps of bread and some cheese. Like Redburn earlier, they are too hungry to eat much, and he is almost sorry he has tried to "prolong their misery" (p. 183).

As effective as Redburn's outcry is against society's indifference to the poor, that is secondary to what the episode suggests about the general human condition. Here, as in several other places throughout the book, physical hunger symbolizes spiritual hunger. People may starve in various ways. That is the essential truth revealed in Redburn's total experience. Constantly he is exposed to one form of starvation or the other. Jackson, the most malicious member of the *Highlander*'s crew, never wants for food, but he is dying of malnutrition just as surely as the woman in Launcelott's-Hey. He has been described as "the first of several persons in Melville's books who embody the principle of absolute evil."[13] In delineating Jackson, however, Melville does not fail to make him human, for as Redburn sees, Jackson's fatal illness, which makes him weaker and weaker like a man who is famishing, is the outward manifestation of a human soul in the agony of starvation. Early in the book he is described as "all the time rubbing his back," as if he has an itch or a pain he cannot get to (p. 80).

Redburn therefore sees more in Jackson than simply "the principle of absolute evil." Jackson's plight is reflected in the episode involving a wrecked ship which the *Highlander* encounters while crossing the Grand Banks. As they pass the wreck, the crew of the *Highlander* sees the bodies of three sailors who had lashed themselves to the taffrail for safety in a storm and then, as Redburn conjectures, "famished." These starved sailors furnish the occasion for Jackson to taunt Redburn and to ask him viciously how he would like the same fate. Ironically it is Jackson who is famishing, as his outcries to Blunt indicate. His renunciation of

13. Tyrus Hillway, *Herman Melville* (New York, 1963), p. 73.

39

heaven sounds like the outraged protestations of a man in spiritual agony, a man who wants and needs God but who can believe in nothing:

> Don't talk of heaven to me—it's a lie—I know it—and they are all fools that believe in it. Do you think, you Greek, that there's any heaven for *you*? Will they let *you* in there, with that tarry hand, and that oily head of hair? Avast! when some shark gulps you down his hatchway one of these days, you'll find, that by dying, you'll only go from one gale of wind to another; mind that, you Irish cockney! Yes, you'll be bolted down like one of your own pills: and I should like to see the whole ship swallowed down in the Norway maelstrom, like a box on 'em. (p. 104)

Throughout the voyage Jackson seems to have one main goal, to protest violently against heaven and earth: "During the long night watches, [he] would enter into arguments, to prove that there was nothing to be believed; nothing to be loved, and nothing worth living for; but every thing to be hated, in the wide world" (p. 104). The spectacle of human starvation always arouses in Redburn a deep sense of pity: "But there seemed even more woe than wickedness about the man; and his wickedness seemed to spring from his woe; and for all of his hideousness, there was that in his eye at times, that was ineffably pitiable and touching; and though there were moments when I almost hated this Jackson, yet I have pitied no man as I have pitied him" (p. 105). Redburn experienced the pangs of psychological hunger in himself early enough to recognize that form of suffering in another human being. The evil hunger as well as the good.

If Redburn pitied no man as he did Jackson, he came very close to it with his feeling for Harry Bolton. Looking back on Harry, he exclaims: "Poor Harry! a feeling of sadness, never to be comforted, comes over me, even now when I think of you" (p. 252). It was sadness that came from a realization that Harry Bolton was dying of the same ailment as Jackson. When he tells Redburn that "I won't sing for my mutton" (p. 280), Harry is in a sense announcing his spiritual starvation as well as his literal ineptness at making a living. Singing is his only real talent, and when he refuses to do that and, later, joins the crew of a whaler, he in effect commits suicide. Redburn learns years after his first voyage that Harry had died at sea by falling from his ship.

Significantly Jackson died the same way. The two men are externally as different as possible. Jackson is crude, malicious, and base in every way. The "Bury blade" is a refined dandy, generous to a fault. Yet it is clear that they have in common a terrible hollowness. They are both desperate men with deep and mysterious cravings who live lives without apparent purpose or aim. The sailor who informs Redburn of Harry's death inquires: "Harry Bolton was not your brother?" (p. 312). Redburn does not record what answer he made, but remarks simply: "*Harry Bolton!* it was even he!" (p. 312). In a limited sense Harry was Redburn's brother and so was Jackson because Redburn, too, "had been hungry all the years."

To say that Redburn senses the torment in these men and pities them deeply is not, however, to say that he is like them.[14] Despite his affection for Harry, Redburn feels constantly alienated from him. The problem is basically that Harry is not what he seems—or, rather, that beneath his sparkling exterior of refined manners

14. For an opposing view of Redburn, see H. Bruce Franklin, "Redburn's Wicked End," *Nineteenth-Century Fiction*, xx (1965), 190–94. Franklin depicts Redburn as somewhat wicked for leaving Harry Bolton: "Redburn becomes the incarnation of all he has learned to fear and despise. . . . [He] completes his loss of innocence and initiation into guilt—by betraying Harry Bolton . . ." (p. 191). For another unsympathetic view of Redburn, see Terrence G. Lish, "Melville's *Redburn*: A Study in Dualism," *English Language Notes*, v (1967), 113–20. Like Franklin, Lish blames Redburn for leaving Bolton: "In clutching his innocence to his breast, [he] . . . earns the reader's contempt." Lish concludes that "In presenting Redburn as an unsympathetic figure, Melville would seem to criticize all those on whatever stratum of being who elect to retain their innocence and submit to a superimposed will at the cost of relinquishing their brotherhood with mankind" (p. 120). John Seelye gives Redburn credit for learning and improving his character, but feels that his farewell to Harry shows that "still he remains essentially a prig at heart." See *Melville: The Ironic Diagram* (Evanston, 1970), p. 52. Seelye also refers to Redburn as a "fatuous ass" who "grasps only the obvious" (p. 163).

and carefree love of life, some disturbing secret is faintly discernible. Redburn can never overcome his "suspicions concerning the rigid morality" of Harry "as a teller of the truth" (p. 223). He tries very hard to put aside his reservations about his friend, "yet, spite of all this, I never could entirely digest some of his imperial reminiscences of high life. I was very sorry for this; as at times it made me feel ill at ease in his company; and made me hold back my whole soul from him; when, in its loneliness, it was yearning to throw itself into the unbounded bosom of some immaculate friend" (p. 223).

Harry is thus a shadow without recognizable substance. Redburn—and the reader—can believe very little that he says. He lies, for example, about having gone to sea as a boy. He is running away from something when Redburn meets him, but what precisely is it? And what is the purpose of Redburn's frequent references to Harry's "feminine" complexion, "womanly" eyes, and small feet ("like a doll's")? It is not at all clear that Melville wanted to depict him as a sexual deviate, although many signs point in that direction. At any rate, mystery prevails in every aspect of his characterization from his background to his hormones. Redburn is struck with the difference between Harry's delightful external exuberance and the disturbingly false notes that reverberate from the recesses of his mind. One fact that can be determined about Harry's inner life is that his hunger is intense. An outward sign of this desperate craving is his incurable desire to gamble. It did not take him long to lose his handsome inheritance "in the company of gambling sportsmen and dandies" (p. 217). The crew of the *Highlander* speculate endlessly about Harry, but the one thing they all seem to be sure of is that "by abandoning his country, Harry had left more room for the gamblers" (p. 254). Exactly what occurs in that strange place in London called "Aladdin's Palace" is difficult to say, but it is apparent that Harry loses—probably by gambling—nearly all the money he has left. When Redburn accuses him of gambling, Harry reacts almost hysterically because Redburn has unconsciously reminded him of an emptiness which cannot be filled: " 'Ha, ha,' he deliriously laughed. 'Gambling? red and white, you mean?—cards?—dice?—the bones?—Ha, ha!—Gambling? gambling?' he ground out between his teeth—'what two devilish, stiletto-sounding syllables they are!' " (pp. 234–35). The empty purse which he flings down before Redburn is a symbol of his hollow being. "That's about all that's left of me," he tells Redburn. "That's my skeleton" (p. 235).

In an otherwise clear, direct, and unadorned narrative the chapter on Redburn and Harry in Aladdin's Palace stands out starkly. From the grimy forecastle of the *Highlander* Redburn is suddenly transported to a setting of almost unbelievable elegance (in his mind), where he has only the faintest idea of what is transpiring around him. The hunger so much in evidence on the sordid streets of Liverpool seems far away. Yet in truth it is not, for Aladdin's Palace is very much a contributing part to the depiction of that other kind of hunger, psychological rather than physical, which is present in many of the characters in *Redburn*. The description of Aladdin's Palace constitutes a highly imaginative and elaborate metaphor for Harry Bolton. To read Redburn's account of the strange gambling house is to see projected concretely all that he senses about Harry.

The only time in the novel when Harry seems in harmony with his setting is when he is in Aladdin's Palace. In fact he refers to it as "home" to Redburn, who takes him at his word and asks, "And pray, do you live here, Harry, in this Palace of Aladdin?" (p. 231). It is, indeed, his "home"; it is his proper sphere because Harry is himself a kind of Aladdin's Palace. On the surface it seems a place of gaiety and sophistication, a "place of opulent entertainment," which Redburn says "far surpassed any thing of the kind I had ever seen before" (p. 228). Harry struck him in the same way. But Redburn in describing his discomfort in Aladdin's Palace is also expressing his suspicions about Harry: when one trod over the floor, he writes, it echoed "as if all the Paris catacombs were underneath. I started with misgivings at that hollow, boding sound, which seemed sighing with a subterraneous despair,

43

through all the magnificent spectacle around me; mocking it, where most of it glared" (p. 228). The contrast of "golden splendor" and "subterraneous despair," ever present in Redburn's description of Aladdin's Palace, is the duality he sees in Harry. He does not know what it is, but Redburn is sure that there is something badly wrong with Harry much as there seems to be some secret evil lying below the surface of Aladdin's Palace. Throughout the chapter Redburn uses such words as "mysterious" and "strange" to describe his reaction to the place. It is as "unaccountable" to him as is Harry's conduct.

Aladdin's Palace, then, functions as an epiphany—for the reader if not for Redburn himself. Through the image of the gambling house, one sees the image of Harry Bolton, and two things are very clear. The first is that below Harry's gay exterior lies a pitifully starved soul. But it also becomes clear that if Redburn is drawn to Harry because he pities him and sympathizes with his insulted sensibilities and his frustrated hunt for the unattainable, still there is an element of mysterious evil in Harry that Redburn does not share or understand. At one point Redburn describes his intuitions about Aladdin's Palace in such a manner as to suggest his fears about Harry, fears that are half articulated in other places.[15] "But spite of these thoughts, and spite of the metropolitan magnificence around me, I was mysteriously alive to a dreadful feeling, which I had never before felt, except when penetrating into the lowest and most squalid haunts of sailor iniquity in Liverpool. All the mirrors and marbles around me seemed crawling over with lizards; and I thought to myself, that though gilded and golden, the serpent of vice is a serpent still" (p. 234). The serpent imagery of this passage recurs in other places in the description of Aladdin's Palace. For example, the oriental ottomans are "wrought into plaited serpents,

15. In Chapter 45, for example, Redburn says: "I asked him why he had gone to that unnecessary expense, when he had plenty of other clothes in his chest. But he only winked, and looked knowing. This, again, I did not like. But I strove to drown ugly thoughts" (p. 225).

undulating beneath beds of leaves," with flashing "splendors of green scales and gold" (p. 230). There is also a marble bracket "sculptured in the semblance of a dragon's crest" (p. 231). The same imagery in Aladdin's Palace that suggests a side of Harry Bolton's nature is used to describe Jackson, who has "cold, and snaky" eyes (p. 57).[16] Redburn comments that "the blue hollows of his eyes were like vaults full of snakes" (p. 295).[17]

Like all of Melville's early heroes Redburn is basically honest and incorruptible. Although strongly drawn toward Harry, he is ultimately alienated from him as he is from Jackson.[18] Melville is expressing more than a casual difference between Redburn and Harry when he shows their opposite reactions to sailing and to climbing aloft. Harry falsely claims to be "an expert tumbler in the . . . rigging" (p. 220), but actually finds every aspect of life at sea repulsive. He is totally incapable of going aloft. Redburn, on the other hand, responds to the ship: "Every mast and timber seemed to have a pulse in it that was beating with life and joy; and I felt a wild

16. As Jackson grows more ill, "his snaky eyes rolled in red sockets" (p. 275).

17. The horror of all these references is enhanced by the application of snake imagery to the fire that plays over the face of the dead Miguel: "Two threads of greenish fire, like a forked tongue, darted out between the lips; and in a moment, the cadaverous face was crawled over by a swarm of worm-like flames" (p. 244).

18. Edgar A. Dryden, in *Melville's Thematics of Form* (Baltimore, 1968), argues that Redburn is afraid of becoming another Jackson and thus writes the book as a confession of having denied his "brother," Harry Bolton (p. 67). See also James Schroeter, *"Redburn* and the Failure of Mythic Criticism," *American Literature*, xxxix (1967), 279–97. Schroeter, unlike Dryden, does not see Redburn as guilt-ridden, but indicates that he might have become another Jackson or Bolton: "The figures are orbits, either one of which Redburn might have been drawn into with disastrous consequences" (p. 294). These orbits Schroeter finds much like the "aristocratic" and "plebeian" attitudes "which Melville avoids in narrating the book" (p. 294). My contention is that Redburn is never really tempted to be like Jackson or Bolton and that no suspense at all is created in the story over such a possibility. Furthermore, I see no evidence that Redburn feels guilty about leaving Harry at the end.

exulting in my own heart . . ." (p. 66). The following passage, in which Redburn expresses his feelings about working in the rigging, should be read as a background to Harry's refusal to go aloft because "*his nerves could not stand it*" (pp. 255–56):

> I took great delight in furling the top-gallant sails and royals in a hard blow; which duty required two hands on the yard.
> There was a wild delirium about it; a fine rushing of the blood about the heart; and a glad thrilling and throbbing of the whole system, to find yourself tossed up at every pitch into the clouds of a stormy sky, and hovering like a judgment angel between heaven and earth; both hands free, with one foot in the rigging, and one somewhere behind you in the air. The sail would fill out like a balloon, with a report like a small cannon, and then collapse and sink away into a handful. And the feeling of mastering the rebellious canvas, and tying it down like a slave to the spar, and binding it over and over with the *gasket,* had a touch of pride and power in it, such as young King Richard must have felt, when he trampled down the insurgents of Wat Tyler. (pp. 115–16)

If Aladdin's Palace is Harry's "home," this is Redburn's—or, rather, the closest he or any other of Melville's heroes can come to having a home.

In *Redburn*, then, the narrator makes his way through a kind of jungle of hunger. He sees it in the streets of Liverpool, where women are "drying up with slow starvation" and where pathetic young men sit with signs:

> *I have had no food for three days;*
> *My wife and children are dying.*

He sees it among the hundreds of Irish emigrants on board the *Highlander* on its return trip. He experienced it himself in New York before departing for Liverpool. He recognizes another kind of hunger, too, and sees it manifested in men as different as Jackson, Harry Bolton, and Blunt (who seeks sustenance through the *Bona-*

46

parte Dream Book). More importantly Redburn feels it deep within himself—as different as he is from them.[19]

He is not merely an observer on this safari through hunger, therefore. He is himself a hunter. This role is suggested at the very beginning when his brother offers him a shooting-jacket and a rifle to take along on his journey. He pawns the rifle in New York but wears the uncomfortable jacket throughout. It is scarcely the appropriate garment, however, for the kind of hunter he is. He hunts, or seeks, not for sport but because he hungers. But the jacket and the pantaloons he wears ("made in the height of sporting fashion") make him absurd in the eyes of the officers and men. Sarcastically Captain Riga exclaims: "You are quite a sportsman I see" (p. 17). Besides the irony of calling a man a "sportsman" because he hunts from hunger, there is further irony because the hunter is also hunted. From the moment he pawns his rifle to buy a bright red shirt, he becomes a kind of fox, being hunted for *others'* "sport." His jacket, in fact, has large buttons, "upon each of which was a carved fox" (p. 17). And it is by the name "Buttons" that he goes while on the *Highlander*. Buttons (or the fox) is sought out heartlessly by the crew to scold or tease. Ironically a man in Liverpool stops Redburn on the dock to inquire whether *he* is going fox-hunting! (p. 153).

The hunter-hunted paradox is further developed through various references to traps. When Redburn first comes aboard the *Highlander*, he encounters a sailor who takes a look at his jacket and asks sarcastically if he has brought his "traps aboard" (p. 24). More often than not, however, he feels less like the trapper than the trapped. The numerous advertisements which he sees on the dock walls of Liverpool are designed to take in the unwary. There

19. As a part of the complex motif of hunger, food is mentioned and described in a great number of places. Handsome Mary's Sunday dinners at the Baltimore Clipper, for example, are abundant and tasty: "The roast beef of Old England abounded; and so did the immortal plum-puddings, and the unspeakably capital gooseberry pies" (p. 204).

are grand-sounding announcements of available berths on *"superior, fast-sailing, coppered and copper-fastened ships"* departing for various places over the globe, and "interspersed with these, are the advertisements of Jewish clothesmen, informing the judicious seaman where he can procure of the best and the cheapest; together with ambiguous medical announcements of the tribe of quacks and empirics who prey upon all seafaring men" (p. 192). These and other such appeals strike Redburn as subtle kinds of traps. "I never passed these advertisements, surrounded by crowds of gaping emigrants," he says, "without thinking of rat-traps" (p. 194).

He finds traps everywhere, even on his most pleasant excursion, a long ramble through the countryside around Liverpool. As he comes to a reposeful little dale, he considers stopping for a nap but abruptly comes upon "a frightful announcement" nailed to a tree: "MAN-TRAPS AND SPRING-GUNS!" He is momentarily baffled but concludes that "the announcement could bear but one meaning—that there was something near by, intended to catch human beings; some species of mechanism, that would suddenly fasten upon the unwary rover . . ." (p. 210). There is *always* something nearby to catch him. He escapes this particular trap only to be caught in another—Aladdin's Palace. There he is so fascinated with the elaborate surroundings that he cannot leave, though he wishes to. His "fearful reveries," he says, "only enchanted me fast to my chair; so that, though I then wished to rush forth from the house, my limbs seemed manacled" (p. 233).

As a hunter, seeking to alleviate his pangs of hunger, Redburn never finds exactly what he seeks. He discovers instead that experience is the constant assault upon man's sense of the appropriate. Or, to put it another way, that life is made up essentially and in varying degrees of the unexpected. From the time Redburn leaves home to go to sea he is struck with how out of kilter the world seems. Indeed, the main fact of life to which Redburn is constantly forced to respond is not so much the omnipresence of evil—a theme which has been overemphasized in critical commentary on the book[20]—but the phenomenon of the inappropriate. Man's sense of the appropriate is a form of expectation created from past experience—or from what one has heard or read—and modified by the imagination (and sometimes by those inevitable tricks of memory). It is repeatedly being jarred by what one actually encounters. For example, we form ideas and images in connection with the appropriate manners and activities (and sometimes even physical appearances) of different kinds of people. We may think of a physician or a sea captain as conducting himself along certain specific lines. But the chances are that the individual physician or the sea captain that we really encounter will be in some degree different from the abstract and collective one. What happens in *Redburn* is that there is an almost intolerable concentration of inappropriateness bombarding the hero, and he is forced so often to make a necessary psychological adjustment to absorb the incongruous that he sometimes approaches complete frustration. His test is to remain moral and sane under such bombardment—and that Redburn manages to do.

Very little seems "right" to Redburn after he leaves home. The world is upside down. For example, he has formed a sense of what a sea captain *should* be—the appropriate captain. He expects Captain Riga to be a just man, a gentleman who will appreciate a gentleman's son. "I had made no doubt," he says, "that he would in some special manner take me under his protection, and prove a kind friend and benefactor to me; as I had heard that some sea-captains are fathers to their crew" (p. 67). He had visions of the good captain inviting him to dinner and questioning him kindly about his family background. What he actually encountered was a petty, unfeeling tyrant, who could not have cared less for his welfare had he been a barnacle on the hull of the *Highlander*.

With his shooting-jacket and pantaloons Redburn is dressed about as inappropriately for his job as he could be. He does not

20. See, for example, Newton Arvin's section on *Redburn* in *Herman Melville* (New York, 1950), pp. 103–109.

49

have the correct eating utensils, and he suffers much from "going to sea so ill provided" (p. 75). But these discomforts are minor compared to the general disappointment and sometimes bafflement that he undergoes during the entire experience of his first voyage. Everywhere he looks his sense of the appropriate is offended. Whales, he thinks, *should* be monstrous creatures of wonder. When the *Highlander* comes close to a group of whales, however, he sees something far different from what he had anticipated. His reaction to the whales is, in a sense, like the starving woman's reaction to the bread he offered her, or like Tommo's experience at the stream: "Can these be whales? Monstrous whales, such as I had heard of? I thought they would look like mountains on the sea. . . . It was a bitter disappointment, from which I was long in recovering" (p. 96).

Time and again for Redburn the expected fruits of experience turn out to be the bitter apples of Sodom.[21] He had thought the shore of a foreign land would be "something strange and wonderful," but when he first catches a glimpse of Ireland, he finds nothing at all remarkable about it. And the sight of Liverpool crushes him. "To be sure," he says, "I did not expect that every house in Liverpool must be a Leaning Tower of Pisa, or a Strasbourg Cathedral; but yet, these edifices I must confess, were a sad and bitter disappointment to me" (p. 127).

One reason why man's sense of the appropriate is constantly

---

21. Melville was greatly impressed with a passage from Book X of *Paradise Lost*:

> . . . Greedily they pluck'd
> the Frutage fair to sight, like that which grew
> Neer that bituminous Lake where *Sodom* flam'd;
> This more delusive, not the touch, but taste
> Deceav'd; they fondly thinking to allay
> Thir appetite with gust, instead of Fruit
> Chewd bitter Ashes, which th' offended taste
> With spattering noise rejected. . . . (Lines 560–67)

For Milton's influence on Melville, see Henry F. Pommer, *Milton and Melville* (Pittsburgh, 1950).

offended is that "this world," as Redburn puts it, "is a moving world . . . ; it never stands still; and its sands are forever shifting" (p. 157).[22] In this process of change or flux, which is the essence of life, the human mind usually remains a step behind. Man's mind demands permanence but encounters motion and change; it categorizes and types but finds only variations. This is the truth embodied in Redburn's experience with his father's guidebook. When he sailed, he took along two books, Smith's *The Wealth of Nations*, which Mr. Jones had given him in New York, and *The Picture of Liverpool*, a guidebook which his father had used a half-century earlier when he had visited England. What Redburn discovers about the first book prepares for the more significant episode involving the guidebook. He hoped *The Wealth of Nations* would serve, as Mr. Jones suggested, as a guidebook to lead him to "the true way to retrieve the poverty of my family, and again make them all well to do in the world" (p. 86). What he had anticipated would be "like the philosopher's stone, a secret talisman," turned out to be "dry as crackers and cheese" (pp. 86, 87). The book has no relevance for him. Turning it over, he discovers that it had originally belonged to Mr. Jones's father. From the amount of dust on the book, it is clear that the young Jones found as little use for *The Wealth of Nations* as Redburn did.

Thus Redburn's disappointment with his own father's guidebook is foreshadowed. He had read the guidebook and cherished it because it had served his father, and from it he had formed a picture of Liverpool in his mind—a sense of the appropriate insofar as Liverpool was concerned. But here, as in numerous other places, he does not find what he expects. With much irony and seeming mock admiration, he spends an entire chapter describing in almost

---

22. Charles Feidelson, Jr., makes the point succinctly in *Symbolism and American Literature* (Chicago, 1953): "The only reality, therefore, lies in the process of becoming; not in the illusory permanence of guidebooks but in the hazards of change. Redburn is the voyaging consciousness. . . . At Liverpool he becomes aware of what he has learned: that the meaning of the voyage lies precisely in change of meaning" (p. 180).

minute detail the physical appearance and contents of the old guidebook. As the chapter proceeds, however, it becomes clear that his tone is not really mockery and that this is more than just a familiar book to him—the guidebook is entangled with his own past to such an extent that it has become very personal to him. In it he sees his father's notes; it represents a segment of his father's life and personality. He traces his father's activities through these notes and tries to visit the same places in Liverpool. In the guide-book he also sees evidence of "the handiwork of my brothers, and sisters, and cousins; and the hands that sketched some of them are now moldered away" (p. 143). There, too, are his own juvenile scribblings and drawings. So much of himself and his family is in the book that as he looks at it, he seems to "melt into the past and forgotten!" (p. 143).

The tone in which the guidebook is described is highly signif-icant, for it suggests Redburn's attitude not only toward that book but also toward his youth, his great expectations, and the general world picture which he had when he took his first voyage. "I am filled," he writes, "with a comical sadness" (p. 149). It is both comic and sad that he could have been so wrong in his expectations—that the sum total of his childhood adds up to so little that is meaningful and useful as he confronts the world. His father's experience cannot be his own. His childhood dreams and the sheltered and loving guidance of his family are now as worthless as the fifty-year-old guidebook, in which they are reflected.

Redburn's testing of the guidebook is thus a testing of many of his ideas of the appropriate—ideas formed from others' experience. As he goes from one place to another in Liverpool, trying to follow the guidebook and retrace his father's steps, he finds time and again that the buildings he seeks have been torn down or replaced with others. What *should* be a fort has become a tavern; Riddough's Hotel, where his father stayed *should* still be there, but it has been demolished; what *should* be the Old Dock is now the customs house; and although the Abbey of Birkenhead *should* be easy to locate, it seems to have "mysteriously disappeared."

The purpose of the guidebook section in *Redburn* is to make one of Melville's most insistent points: man has very little in life which he can depend on to guide him infallibly as he encounters new experiences. His family background, his past, all the dogmas and creeds of the world—none will give him all the answers, none will tell him what Liverpool is really like. He must go there himself, and when he does, he will find that it is not a perfect copy of the Liverpool he had pictured in his mind. And if he leaves and returns, he will find that it is not exactly as he remembered it. Melville uses the guidebook, then, as a symbol for all that goes to make up man's sense of the appropriate:

> It was a sad, a solemn, and a most melancholy thought. The book on which I had so much relied; the book in the old morocco cover; the book with the cocked-hat corners; the book full of fine old family associations; the book with seventeen plates, executed in the highest style of art; this precious book was next to useless. Yes, the thing that had guided the father, could not guide the son. And I sat down on a shop step, and gave loose to meditation. (p. 157)

What he meditates on is the nature and meaning of experience. In this "moving world," the Riddough's Hotels "are forever being pulled down":

> This very harbor of Liverpool is gradually filling up, they say; and who knows what your son (if you ever have one) may behold, when he comes to visit Liverpool, as long after you as you come after his grandfather. And, Wellingborough, as your father's guidebook is no guide for you, neither would yours (could you afford to buy a modern one to-day) be a true guide to those who come after you. Guide-books, Wellingborough, are the least reliable books in all literature; and nearly all literature, in one sense, is made up of guide-books. (p. 157)

Guidebooks take numerous forms but none is entirely reliable, not even man's own built-in mental guidebook—his sense of the appropriate. He is constantly forming ideas and images of what is

53

or should be only to discover over and over again in the shifting sands of experience that his guidebook is perpetually outdated.

The guidebook episode is the intellectual center of *Redburn*. Into the two chapters that deal with *The Picture of Liverpool* and Redburn's discovery of its fallibility, Melville has concentrated his essential philosophy of experience. There are two central episodes in the book; the other one—which could be called the emotional center—is the passage describing the starving family in Launcelott's-Hey. Both episodes are preceded and prepared for by an earlier similar occurrence. Redburn's own discovery of what it means to be so hungry he cannot eat foreshadows the incident in Launcelott's-Hey, and his failure to find Smith's *The Wealth of Nations* meaningful prepares the way for his disappointment with his father's guidebook.

These two central experiences, therefore, represent peaks in the development of two aspects of the same theme. The same essential truth is embodied in Melville's treatment of unsatisfied human hunger as in his development of the difference between expectation and experience. Redburn has in one sense received an education during his first voyage. But in another sense, he is not "initiated" at all because man *cannot* be initiated. He may know very well at the end of the book that he shall always hunger after something he will never taste; he may realize that experience violates almost constantly his sense of what *should* be, from small details to great ideals; but he will continue to hunger and seek because he cannot do otherwise. Such is the nature of the early heroes of Melville.

THE INDEPENDENCE OF SEA

Part II

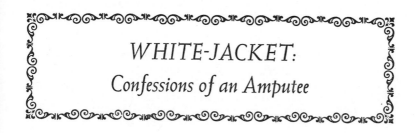

WHITE-JACKET:
Confessions of an Amputee

Chapter 4

W*hite-Jacket* is among other things an autobiographical account of Melville's term aboard the man-of-war *United States* from August 1843 to October 1844. It is partially an indignant outcry against injustices practiced in the U. S. Navy at that time. It is written from a Christian and humanitarian viewpoint. It is also a book about the presence of evil in the world. But even more important, it is an extremely personal account of what it means to acquire manhood.

Manhood for Melville was not merely a matter of reaching one's twenty-first birthday. Indeed, he did not himself come of age, he wrote his friend Hawthorne, until he was twenty-five: "Until I was twenty-five, I had no development at all. From my twenty-fifth year I date my life."[1] Significantly he reached his twenty-fifth birthday toward the end of his voyage aboard the *United States*. In *White-Jacket* he dramatized this event near the end of the book by the narrator's plunge from the main top into the sea. Like several

1. *The Letters of Herman Melville*, ed. Merrell R. Davis and William H. Gilman (New Haven, 1960), p. 130.

important events in *White-Jacket* this one was the product of Melville's imagination, not his actual experience. That is as it should be, for *White-Jacket*, like *Billy Budd*, is essentially "an inside narrative." The heart of the book is not what it says about society, or the injustices of the navy, or democracy, but what it says about one man, White-Jacket. Any sound interpretation of the book must ultimately deal with the inner life of the narrator.

In tracing White-Jacket's change, we see one of the most difficult problems arise from the fact that his fall from the yardarm, which has often been treated by critics as a kind of baptism, comes so close to the end of the story that very little is seen of White-Jacket afterwards. If he has undergone a change, how can it be proved? Our glimpse of him after his fall is very brief. In the few pages that remain he is fished from the sea, and he climbs right back aloft; then he reaches his destination and is discharged. In other words, if we are supposed to see a "before and after" portrait here, there seems precious little to base the "after" side on. Yet White-Jacket's plunge was obviously intended as the central symbolic episode of the book, and although little is seen of him thereafter, one must necessarily assume some change.

The actual problem, however, is not precisely as I have stated it, for it is not White-Jacket after his fall who is difficult to delineate, but the earlier White-Jacket. The voice heard from the first page onward is that of the matured White-Jacket relating his experiences on the *Neversink*. We can see what he has become; the difficulty comes in trying to see what he was before and during the events of the narrative. That portrait has to be pieced together from bits and fragments and hints scattered throughout most of the book.

One of the means by which the younger and older White-Jacket are juxtaposed is through the use of doubles. They offer an extremely helpful means of determining the difference between White-Jacket before he acquired manhood and afterwards, or, to put it differently, of determining the meaning of manhood.

The first set consists of Williams and Nord, who are both among the few close friends of the narrator. They illustrate the primary differences between the earlier and later White-Jacket. Williams, a "thorough-going Yankee," "had been both a peddler and a pedagogue in his day" (p. 52).[2] Williams's role in the book is that of Youth. He is "honest, acute, witty, full of mirth and good-humor— a laughing philosopher," but he has no depth (p. 52). He talks constantly about his past. Nord, on the other hand, is "a wandering recluse, even among our man-of-war mob" (p. 51). He has depth where Williams has wit, dignity instead of boyishness, seriousness in place of mirth, a certain hardness instead of youthful bounce, and a mysterious independence as opposed to Williams's ties with his past. He is, in short, all that White-Jacket came to admire and respect. Like him, Nord admires Montaigne. White-Jacket can give him no higher praise than to assume "he seized the right meaning of Montaigne" (p. 51). For these reasons White-Jacket is strongly drawn to him: "I saw that he was an earnest thinker; I more than suspected that he had been bolted in the mill of adversity. For all these things my heart yearned toward him; I determined to know him" (p. 51). During a midnight watch "White-Jacket learned more than he has ever done in any single night since" (p. 51). He is amazed that Nord has preserved his dignity among "such a rabble rout" as the crew. His admiration grows as he observes the respect which even the officers have for Nord. A lonely figure among men, Nord has apparently cut himself off from his past: "He was barred and locked up like the specie vaults of the Bank of England. For any thing that dropped from him, none of us could be sure that he had ever existed till now. Altogether, he was a remarkable man" (p. 52). These two men, Williams and Nord, reflect the differences between what White-Jacket was and what he becomes. The one is youthful, alive with the past; the other, older than his years, a "diver" into questions of human existence. The voyage of the *Neversink* around Cape Horn

2. An actual friend of Melville's on board the *United States*, Griffith Williams must have reminded Melville of himself in several ways. He, too, had been a "peddler" in his brother's store, and for a while he was a teacher.

("there is some sort of a Cape Horn for all," White-Jacket says) to the Atlantic is the journey White-Jacket takes from Williams to Nord. Foreshadowing the dominance in White-Jacket of Nord-like attributes and the destruction of Williams-like youth and exuberance, Chapter 13 ends with this remark: "I introduced them to each other; but *Nord cut him dead* the very same evening, when we sallied out from between the guns for a walk on the main-deck" (p. 52, italics mine).

The difference between what the narrator was and is can again be seen in a later chapter, "A Man-of-War Button Divides Two Brothers." This time White-Jacket himself is one of the characters, but it is the other character, Frank, who represents the narrator when he was younger. In recounting the conversation between the two characters, the narrator, for sake of contrast, depicts himself more as what he has since become than as he was at the time of the event. Frank dreads an imminent encounter with his brother: "I have calculated that the Store Ship may be expected here every day; my brother will then see me—he an officer and I a miserable sailor that any moment may be flogged at the gangway, before his very eyes" (p. 244). The agony of youthful pride is intense. Frank has been away from home about three years, yet he cannot forget his family, and the possibility that he may be degraded in its eyes overwhelms him: "I have been from home nearly three years; in that time I have never heard one word from my family, and, though God knows how I love them, yet I swear to you, that though my brother can tell me whether my sisters are still alive, yet, rather than accost him in this *lined-frock*, I would go ten centuries without hearing one syllable from home!" (p. 244).[3]

3. Frank seems to reflect Melville's own feelings when he discovered the announcement in a New York newspaper that his cousin, Stanwix Gansevoort, had become a midshipman in the United States Navy and was on his way to meet the *United States*, then in Rio, aboard a supply ship. Almost every detail of the incident in *White-Jacket* parallels the actual circumstances. See Wilson L. Heflin, "A Man-of-War Button Divides Two Cousins," *Boston Public Library Quarterly*, III (1951), 51–60. Only a few years his junior, Stanwix was, indeed, like a brother. But more important, Stanwix repre-

White-Jacket's reaction to Frank's fears is that of the man free from such strong family ties. He respects men like Nord, who sever their ties with family and past and who sail independently if perilously in the "howling infinite." He remarks to Frank that if his brother should "give himself airs over you, simply because he sports large brass buttons on his coat ... he can be no brother, and ought to be hanged—that's all!" (p. 244). Frank's angry retort reveals that he has not yet learned the meaning of manhood; his concept of dignity involves the externals of position and status rather than those qualities shown in Nord, Jack Chase, and old Ushant, who are not officers but who nevertheless possess true dignity:

> "Don't say that again," said Frank, resentfully; "my brother is a noble-hearted fellow; I love him as I do myself. You don't understand me, White-Jacket; don't you see, that when my brother arrives, he must consort more or less with our chuckle-headed reefers on board here? There's that namby-pamby Miss Nance of a white-face, Stribbles, who, the other day, when Mad Jack's back was turned, ordered me to hand him the spy-glass, as if he were a Commodore. Do you suppose, now, I want my brother to see me a lackey aboard here? By Heaven, it is enough to drive one distracted!" (p. 244)

In both scenes, the one involving Williams and Nord, the other Frank and White-Jacket, attitudes toward family are important because independence of thought is absolutely essential to manhood. One can not dive deeply if encumbered with the prejudices and false pride that frequently go along with close family ties. The heroes of Melville's work inevitably break away from family to become Ishmaels or Nords or Bulkingtons, lonely men who keep the "open independence of ... sea." Williams and Frank have not

---

sented the family. The Melville-Gansevoort heritage was a noble one, but it was also an albatross about Melville's neck. He could never do what it seemed to expect of him, could never be what it wanted him to be. From his earliest years, he was not allowed to forget that his was a long and proud lineage. His feelings, then, might well have been those attributed to Frank.

yet reached this stage of manhood; White-Jacket does, however. As Lawrance Thompson has pointed out, the tone of White-Jacket's narrative is sometimes marked by a strange cynicism, which unmistakably flows beneath much of the surface piousness. It is the voice of a man who has been deeply affected by what he has seen and thought. He is not, however, quarreling with God, as Thompson asserts, but with all allegiances and dogmas that prevent earnest, independent thought and therefore destroy his chance for manhood and true dignity.

White-Jacket tells very little about his past directly, but he hints that he came from a good family—he is taken aback when the surgeon's assistant asks him if his family was "consumptive." Furthermore, his family background apparently played an influential part in forming his manner and ideas. In fact, it is probably because he has such close family ties that he almost from the first describes life aboard the *Neversink* with family metaphors.[4] He is struck with the similarities between an actual family circle and the relationships on the frigate, but the more he sees the more he realizes that it was a very imperfect family indeed, so that the extended comparison finally becomes bitingly ironic. The midshipmen are children; the senior lieutenant, who sees to it that the midshipmen get to sleep, is "like the father of a numerous family after getting up in his dressing-gown and slippers, to quiet a daybreak tumult in his populous nursery" (p. 26). Captain Claret is "the father of his crew," and has the duty of looking after "his ocean children" (p. 90). Parts of the ship under hatches are "like the gloomy entrances to family vaults of buried dead" (p. 127). The job of the master-at-arms resembles that of a family housekeeper, "ferreting over a rambling old house in the country," to be sure all doors are bolted, all lights out, and the embers in the fireplace smothered (p. 284). References such as these abound. The ship is a home with strict rules that must be followed (the Articles of War); if they are broken, there must be stern punishment (flogging) in order to

---

4. With some frequency the ship is also described as a microcosm.

insure future obedience. Collectively the comparisons function ironically, for life on board the *Neversink* is anything but a harmonious family circle. The "father," Claret, has no real concern for his "children." The "children" are in the main incurably corrupt—not innocent—and the "spankings" they receive for disobedience do not mold character but embitter and scar. The extended metaphor of the family is thus an extremely effective way of pointing up the tyranny, cruelty, and evil that make up "The World in a Man-of-War," as Melville subtitled his book. White-Jacket left his actual family to look for another, larger one. What he finds is a nightmare family, every flaw magnified. Finally he has to break loose from the influence of his real family to be independent, but he comes to realize that when he does there will not be another to take its place. The break, then, is extremely painful.

The symbol for the narrator's real family and its influence on him is his white jacket, which he both hates and cherishes. After describing it in detail in the first chapter, he ends with one of the most significant comparisons in the book: "Such, then, was my jacket: a well-patched, padded, and porous one; and in a dark night, gleaming white, as the White Lady of Avenel!" (p. 5). The allusion is to Scott's novel *The Monastery*, in which the Avenel family possesses a protective ghost or spirit called the "White Lady." Such an influence hovers over White-Jacket—his coat is its symbol—and it remains with him until finally he can cast it off. When he falls from the yardarm in that symbolic plunge into manhood, he is a member of a family no longer. As he falls, he sees his family as if passing in final review: "A bloody film was before my eyes, through which, ghost-like, passed and repassed my father, mother, and sisters" (p. 392).[5] In the water he is freed—not to join another family—but to be a man.

Perhaps the most common view expressed in criticism of this novel is that the jacket represents all that isolates its wearer from the brotherhood of man and that after it is thrown off, the nar-

5. This passage recalls Frank's concern about his sisters in Chapter 59.

rator is then somehow reborn into the arms of humanity. The jacket is thus most frequently seen as solely negative, a dangerous and accursed burden. Such an interpretation depicts White-Jacket as cut off from the crew because of his strange and conspicuous coat, which sets him apart, individualizes him, and keeps him from fitting in harmoniously. He is, then, "a white sheep in the black flock of a man-of-war," as Lewis Mumford puts it.[6] Through the jacket, Ronald Mason states, White-Jacket "acquires nothing but an undeserved ostracism" and when the coat is gone, he experiences a "supreme sense of liberation."[7] Richard Chase calls the jacket "the mark of his alienation."[8] Following Mumford, Charles R. Anderson comments that the jacket made its wearer a "sheep" among "goats."[9] Essentially the same argument has been offered by several critics, who seem to see in the book a movement from personal isolation to redemption through social communion. Howard P. Vincent, for example, states that White-Jacket's isolation results "from his refusal to participate in the ordinary life of humanity"; thus "the friction between White Jacket and the rest of the crew is, symbolically, the opposition between White Jacket and the world at large." With the loss of the jacket, Vincent believes, the Christian paradox of rebirth is realized, and White-Jacket is then a part of the brotherhood of man.[10] Both *Redburn* and *White-Jacket*, argues James E. Miller, Jr., deal with "the gradual dissolution of the barriers separating an isolated individual

6. *Herman Melville: A Study of His Life and Vision*, rev. ed. (New York, 1962), p. 75.

7. *The Spirit Above the Dust* (London, 1951), pp. 92, 93.

8. *Herman Melville: A Critical Study* (New York, 1949), p. 24.

9. *Melville in the South Seas* (New York, 1939), p. 418. Although I disagree with the thrust of Anderson's interpretation, he rightly suggested—though he did not develop—the idea that the jacket "served autobiographically as a coat-of-arms for the Gansevoort-Melville sense of family pride" (p. 418).

10. " 'White Jacket': An Essay in Interpretation," *New England Quarterly*, XXII (1949), 308–309.

from the world."[11] The jacket "makes the wearer a marked man, isolated from the crew." White-Jacket's fall, in Miller's interpretation, is therefore a baptism into humanity.[12]

Melville profoundly respected the isolated thinker and, indeed, insisted that loneliness is inevitable for the searching, sensitive hero. To see White-Jacket moving from a position of isolation to brotherhood is scarcely in keeping with Melville's practice or with evidence from the text itself. There seems to me no indication that White-Jacket is any more a part of the crew or the great world as the novel progresses than he is initially. In fact, near the beginning he tells of feelings of brotherhood which he experienced *early in the voyage* for his fellow maintopmen: "In a large degree, we nourished that feeling of '*esprit de corps*,' always pervading, more or less, the various sections of a man-of-war's crew. We main-top-men were brothers, one and all; and we loaned ourselves to each other with all the freedom in the world" (p. 15). There is no evidence that he ever has more feeling of a sense of common brotherhood than here. Nevertheless White-Jacket remains essentially apart and aloof. After his fall he returns, significantly, to his position aloft, not to the deck to mix with the common crew. With or without the jacket, he can never be one of them.

If there is a change in his degree of isolation, it is toward *less* involvement with the common man, not more. He comes on board the *Neversink* young and inexperienced. He has no aversion to the crew and wants to be one of them. As he sees more and more of the grossness and evil among them and among the officers, he is brought not closer to a position of human brotherhood but further from it. The more he learns of the world the more he realizes his own alienation from it. The jacket plays an important part in this second way of viewing his isolation. Although the jacket certainly does individualize the wearer as numerous critics have pointed out,

11. *A Reader's Guide to Herman Melville* (New York, 1962), p. 67.
12. Ibid., pp. 70, 71.

in a sense it forces him into various relationships that he might not otherwise have. If it makes him appear eccentric in the eyes of the crew, it at least brings him to their attention. It impresses Jack Chase and he forms a friendship with its owner. Shakings seeks out White-Jacket and confides in him how much a man-of-war reminds him of his old cell at Sing-Sing Prison. White-Jacket is before the eyes of the crew and often the subject of their conversation. To individualize is sometimes to make less isolated, not more. Such is the case with the white jacket. However, this is not to argue that the jacket is the symbol of brotherhood, which he loses at the end, for White-Jacket is at *all* times a solitary figure. Instead the proper conclusions seems to be (1) that the narrator does not progress from a state of personal alienation to a position of oneness with common humanity and (2) that the white jacket is far too complex as a symbol to see it merely as a badge of alienation.

That the white jacket is inadequate for the weather, that it stands out and thus causes its wearer to be assigned to more than a normal number of duties, that it is responsible for the narrator's being thrown out of his mess, and that on two occasions it nearly causes his death—these facts make it easy to overlook the positive virtues of the jacket. Yet the narrator makes it clear that the jacket is not without virtues. It is both negative and positive, bad and good. Its very color ought to furnish the necessary hint that Melville is dealing in ambiguity. Though not as complex as the great whale, the white jacket nevertheless comes from the same imaginative source and functions with something of the same ambiguity. If the white whale is more than one thing to Ishmael, the white jacket is more than an albatross to its wearer, and its function in the book is, objectively viewed, constructive as well as destructive. To be sure, it is not much of a coat; it is not waterproof or warm enough, but it *is* a coat, and without it White-Jacket would have frozen. It is a source of pleasure as well as displeasure for him, for "Truly, I thought myself much happier in that white jacket of mine than our old Commodore in his dignified epaulets" (p. 22). When his superstitious messmates force him to leave their mess, he is taken in by a much more desirable group led by Jack Chase. What first appears misfortune turns into good fortune. Even in the scene where the jacket causes him to fall into the sea, hints are given of its ambiguous function. It clearly causes White-Jacket to lose his footing and fall. Furthermore, had he not cut it away in the water, he might have drowned. But at the same time it is quite possible that the jacket saved him. Before this incident another man, Bungs, the ship's cooper, falls from the chains into the sea and is never seen again, despite an extensive search. The explanation offered by Scrimmage, a sheet-anchor man, is that the buoys, which Bungs was himself responsible for making and maintaining, "wouldn't save a drowning man" (p. 73). This incident foreshadows but also contrasts with White-Jacket's plunge, which is from a much greater height but not fatal. Just how large a part the jacket plays in helping him to hit the water without being injured and in retarding his progress downward once in the water cannot, of course, be determined. It is significant, however, that the account in Nathaniel Ames's *A Mariner's Sketches*, on which Melville based White-Jacket's fall, is different in several ways. Ames stated that "I was going aloft and had got as far as the futtock shrouds, when a ratlin broke under my feet and I fell backwards."[13] Melville sends White-Jacket twice as high, beyond the futtock shrouds and even the topmast shrouds, out to the end of the weather-top-gallant yardarm. His fall, then, is no mere repetition of an actual one recorded in Ames. The probability of White-Jacket's coming up from the sea unharmed after falling from a height of one hundred feet is much less than the probability of doing so after a plunge from the futtock shrouds (about fifty feet), from which Ames fell. White-Jacket strikes the water shoulder first, and after being carried down into the sea rises "quicker and quicker" (Ames ascended "slowly") until "I bounded up like a buoy" (p. 393). White-Jacket fell from the yardarm because his jacket flew over his head, "completely muffling" him. As he fell, it must have caught the wind and

13. Quoted in Hennig Cohen, Introduction to *White-Jacket* (New York, 1967), p. xxiii.

thus in the water acted possibly in the same way as Queequeg's coffin in *Moby-Dick*—that is, as a buoy to help bring him quickly to the surface. Bungs drowned because he did not have a proper buoy; White-Jacket is saved, like Ishmael, because of something acting as a buoy. Furthermore, it should be remembered that White-Jacket's fall takes place not in the light of day, but at midnight. The jacket had been described earlier as "gleaming white" on a dark night (p. 5). The crew members who lowered the halyards that dark evening and almost caused White-Jacket to fall from aloft saw only "a moving white spot" (p. 78). Pleading with the first lieutenant for some dark paint, White-Jacket explains: "Consider how it [the jacket] shines of a night, like a bit of the Milky Way" (p. 78). On another occasion White-Jacket complains that in the evenings his coat stands out clearly and causes him to be given extra tasks: "Most monkey jackets are of a dark hue; mine . . . was white. And thus, in those long, dark nights, when it was my quarterwatch on deck, and not in the top, and others went skulking and 'sogering' about the decks, secure from detection—their identity undiscoverable—my own hapless jacket forever proclaimed the name of its wearer" (p. 120). This series of references prepares for White-Jacket's midnight fall. Since the reader has been told so often that the jacket is distinctly visible at night, it comes as no surprise that White-Jacket was spotted quickly in the water and therefore saved.

White-Jacket's attitude toward his strange garment is also ambiguous. Although he curses it, tries to change it, and attempts to get rid of it, he is nevertheless proud of it and strongly attached to it. Just how attached becomes clear when he thinks of giving it to the purser's steward to auction off. He debates the issue with himself at length, thinking of the jacket's loss as a "sacrifice" made "recklessly" (p. 201). Yet he realizes the dangers in keeping it and finally turns it over to the auctioneer. When the crew see it, they respond with surprise and then jeers, leaving no doubts that they consider it perfectly worthless. White-Jacket's reaction to them is very much like Frank's anger when he hears White-Jacket criticize his brother: "While this scene was going forward, and my white jacket was thus being abused, how my heart swelled within me! Thrice was I on the point of rushing out of my hiding-place, and bearing it off from derision" (p. 203). At this point he realizes that his jacket is somehow a part of him and that to dispose of it would be to kill off something of himself: "But no, alas! there was no getting rid of it, except by rolling a forty-two-pound shot in it, and committing it to the deep. But though, in my desperation, I had once contemplated something of that sort, yet I had now become unaccountably averse to it, from certain involuntary superstitious considerations. If I sink my jacket, thought I, it will be sure to spread itself into a bed at the bottom of the sea, upon which I shall sooner or later recline, a dead man" (p. 203).

The jacket is frequently associated with death, but whereas White-Jacket sometimes feels that he will die if he sinks his coat, elsewhere in the book there are suggestions that as long as he wears it he will, in a sense, be dead or unable truly to live. He describes himself as a corpse early in the narrative as he reclines on the main-royal-yard, "the white jacket folded around me like Sir John Moore in his frosted cloak" (p. 77). He is probably alluding to Charles Wolfe's famous elegy, "The Death of Sir John Moore":

> No useless coffin enclosed his breast
>   Not in sheet or in shroud we wound him:
> But he lay like a Warrior taking his rest,
>   With his martial cloak around him.

Immediately after this description of himself aloft in his white jacket, he nearly becomes an actual corpse as the superstitious crewmen below take him for a ghost and almost cause him to fall. This incident recalls, as do several others, the earlier allusion to the jacket as a family ghost, the "gleaming" White Lady of Avernel. In the next chapter White-Jacket again refers to himself as a dead man as he tells of his uncomfortable sleeping conditions: "My luckless hammock was stiff and straight as a board; and there I was—laid out in it, with my nose against the ceiling, like a dead man's against the lid of his coffin" (p. 80). Later he is placed figuratively among the dead when he attempts to offer his coat for auction. Customarily the garments of only deceased mariners are auctioned. Again functioning ambiguously, then, the jacket suggests both an essential element of life, which will bring on death if lost, and a state of death-in-life, which must be set aside in order to live.

Both meanings, however, are compatible with the complex meaning of the jacket in respect to manhood. The gaining of manhood is fraught with ambiguity. To pass from a state of innocence, family influence, and youthful expectations and optimism is to experience both death and life. Some people remain always on the lee shore, never casting off into the "howling infinite" of independent manhood. They retain the jolliness and the undisturbed optimism of death-in-life. Happy Jack is such a character. He has served many years in the navy, but he has never really reached manhood: "He enjoyed life with the zest of everlasting adolescence" (p. 383). He "perpetually wore a hilarious face, and at joke and repartee was a very Joe Miller" (p. 383). His best advice to a young seaman is to be subservient to the officers, "steer clear of all trouble," forget a flogging as soon as possible, and be ready to turn out again for grog. White-Jacket looks upon such a character with feelings akin to Ahab, who says to a happy fellow on one occasion: "Thou art too damned jolly. Sail on."[14] Happy Jack is a favorite among the officers, but to White-Jacket he is "a fellow without shame, without a soul, so dead to the least dignity of manhood that he could hardly be called a man" (p. 384).

Manhood brings death to certain attitudes and youthful sensitivities that are responsible for joy and a sense of wonder in life. Necessary though it is, it is a painful death, and therefore not to be celebrated unequivocally. Toward the end of the book White-Jacket admits sadly that his experiences aboard the *Neversink* have deprived him of his ability to weep over his dead shipmate Shenly.

14. *Moby-Dick*, ed. Harrison Hayford and Hershel Parker (New York, 1967), p. 408.

"This man-of-war life," he confesses, "has not left me unhardened" (p. 345). Like Stephen Crane, Melville held that manhood was purchased with the fine sensibility of youth.[15] Even so, it is far more noble to lose that sensibility than to retain it. To remain untouched, in a sense unhardened, is to be like the soulless Happy Jack, or worse, like Selvagee, an overrefined lieutenant who smells of lavender and sports lace-bordered handkerchiefs. He is soft and unprepared for the gales of life. In contrast another lieutenant, Mad Jack, is "the man who was born in a gale!" (p. 33). Mad Jack has none of Selvagee's refinement. He drinks heavily but keeps his head. The test of his character comes when Captain Claret, also a regular drinker, gives the nearly disastrous order to head the ship away from a storm. Mad Jack counters with an order to meet the storm head-on and thus saves the ship through a maneuver any true student of the sea would know. His is a symbolic action which sums up Melville's position: immerse yourself not in joy or lavender but in the destructive element. That, precisely, is what White-Jacket does.

Through exposure to the destructive element, of which evil is a great part, scales of innocence should fall from the eyes. In the process of attaining manhood, White-Jacket is thrown into the midst of almost every shape and form of evil. If he is left not unhardened, he nevertheless gains an awareness of evil which true manhood demands: an increased depth of insight, a penetrating eye not possessed by the uninitiated. Captain Delano in "Benito Cereno" sees no more after his immersion than before because he

15. In at least two places Melville's concept of courage appears almost identical with Crane's as illustrated in *The Red Badge of Courage*. In Chapter 74, White-Jacket says that courage is the only virtue "shared with us by the beasts of the field" and that "excessive animal courage, in many cases, only finds room in a character vacated of loftier things" (p. 314). In Chapter 75, he comments: "Some man-of-war's-men have confessed to me, that as a battle has raged more and more, their hearts have hardened in infernal harmony; and, like their own guns, they have fought without a thought" (p. 320).

is a kind of child. One of the truest tests of manhood in Melville's works is the ability to penetrate masks or disguises to measure accurately what lies beneath.

In *White-Jacket* the narrator is almost constantly concerned with disguises of various kinds. His fellow sailors, for example, seem "fine fellows! generous-hearted tars!" when they reach shore and begin to spend their earnings. But White-Jacket has learned that the nobility and generosity which *seem* to be there are mere masks: "A man-of-war's man is only a man-of-war's-man at sea; and the sea is the place to learn what he is." There are a few "fine fellows here and there, yet, upon the whole, [a man-of-war is] charged to the combings of her hatchways with the spirit of Belial and all unrighteousness" (p. 390). The satanic master-at-arms, Bland, wears the guise of a perfect gentleman, but White-Jacket penetrates the facade: "I could not but abominate him when I thought of his conduct; but I pitied the continual gnawing which, under all his deftly-donned disguises, I saw lying at the bottom of his soul" (p. 188). The officers are equally disguised. With the exception of Mad Jack they feel compelled to "ship their quarter-deck faces" in order to exert their authority over the crew. They think like young Frank, who is convinced that his brother's button of rank has somehow transformed him into a different and superior creature. The commodore wears his epaulets and commands the greatest respect of all, but beneath the uniform of exalted position is a wilted, ineffectual human being. The chaplain similarly wears the disguise of office. Outwardly he is a spokesman for the Prince of Peace, but actually he is subservient to the god of war: "How can it be expected that the religion of peace should flourish in an oaken castle of war? How can it be expected that the clergyman, whose pulpit is a forty-two pounder, should convert sinners to a faith that enjoins them to turn the right cheek when the left is smitten?" (p. 157). The "Professor," a pedant of naval warfare, professes nothing of true value.

True manhood is not under any of these disguises The most frightening example of the difference between disguise and reality,

however, is the physician, Surgeon Cuticle. His station in life as a
h⌐aler suggests understanding and compassion, but in reality he
is soulless:

> But notwithstanding his marvelous indifference to the sufferings
> of his patients, and spite even of his enthusiasm in his vocation—
> not cooled by frosting old age itself—Cuticle, on some occasions,
> would affect a certain disrelish of his profession, and declaim
> against the necessity that forced a man of his humanity to perform
> a surgical operation. Especially was it apt to be thus with him,
> when the case was one of more than ordinary interest. In discuss-
> ing it, previous to setting about it, he would vail his eagerness
> under an aspect of great circumspection, curiously marred, how-
> ever, by continual sallies of unsuppressible impatience. But the
> knife once in his hand, the compassionless surgeon himself, undis-
> guised, stood before you. Such was Cadwallader Cuticle, our
> Surgeon of the Fleet. (p. 251)

The detailed description of Cuticle's amputation of a crewman's
leg is a masterpiece of horror. Cuticle has no feeling for his patient; his only concern is professional. More and more as he prepares for the operation the true Cuticle becomes evident until he
stands naked before the reader, foul and heartless. One by one his
disguises are removed: first he takes off the coat of his uniform,
then his neckerchief. "These articles being removed, he snatched
off his wig, placing it on the gun-deck capstan; then took out his
set of false teeth, and placed it by the side of the wig; and, lastly,
putting his forefinger to the inner angle of his blind eye, spirted
out the glass optic with professional dexterity, and deposited that,
also, next to the wig and false teeth" (p. 258). What remains when
the disguises of all sorts are removed is "the withered, shrunken,
one-eyed, toothless, hairless Cuticle; with a trunk half dead—a
memento mori to behold!" (p. 259). Throughout the description
of the operation and Cuticle's lecture to his fellow surgeons and
their assistants, the narrator is himself performing an amputation—
systematically he severs Cuticle from the body of humanity.

Disguises can be maintained only as long as they are not sub-

jected to what White-Jacket calls "a manhood-testing conjuncture."
When the captain bursts from his cabin and confusedly gives the
foolish order which Mad Jack contradicts, White-Jacket sees him
without his mask: "That night, off the pitch of the Cape, Captain
Claret was hurried forth from his disguises, and, at a manhood-
testing conjuncture, appeared in his true colors" (p. 111). Beneath
the trappings of manhood there is only weakness, shallowness, and
incompetence. Part of the captain's disguise is his beard, traditionally a symbol of manliness. Toward the end of the voyage
Claret decides at last to have the crew cut their beards in accord
with naval regulations. In speculating about Claret's waiting so
long to give an order about the beards, White-Jacket says: "Perhaps the Captain's generosity in thus far permitting our beards
sprung from the fact that he himself wore a small speck of a beard
upon his own imperial cheek; which, if rumor said true, was to
hide something, as Plutarch relates of the Emperor Adrian. But,
to do him justice—as I always have done—the Captain's beard did
not exceed the limits prescribed by the Navy Department" (p. 356).
In doing him "justice," White-Jacket by implication levels the most
serious charge of all against Claret's manhood, for the Emperor
Adrian (or Hadrian) was well known for his homosexuality.[16]

Beards become more and more significant toward the end of
White-Jacket. Claret's slight regulation beard is a form of disguise.
White-Jacket, Jack Chase, and other members of the crew, however, consider their beards, grown full with the voyage, symbols of
a long and trying experience aboard the *Neversink*. When they are

16. Melville seems to have been mistaken in his reference to Plutarch. I
can find no comment on the Emperor Adrian (or Hadrian) in Plutarch's
writings. More than likely, Melville confused Plutarch with another book of
"lives," the *Historia Augusta*. The life of Hadrian in this work, which is attributed to Aelius Spartianus, contains the following statement: ". . . he
[Hadrian] wore a full beard to cover up the natural blemishes on his face
. . ." (*The Scriptores Historiae Augustae*, trans. David Magie, London, 1922,
I, 79). While this is the specific detail Melville is probably referring to, he
would not have failed to realize another and deeper blemish which the beard
covered.

ordered to cut their beards, they react with resentment, for they feel that they have earned them through endurance. A near-mutiny results, but finally even the oldest tars begin to give up their beards to the ship's barbers. To one crew member in particular his beard becomes so intimately related to personal identity that to remove it would be to lose his dignity and independence—his manhood. This seaman, old Ushant, is captain of the forecastle, "a fine specimen of a sea sexagenarian" (p. 353). Unlike the commodore and Surgeon Cuticle, whose advanced age reflects a wilted soul, Ushant has retained his manhood, and his beard is its symbol, "a wide, spreading beard, grizzled and gray, that flowed over his breast, and often became tangled and knotted with tar" (p. 353). Every detail of White-Jacket's description of Ushant points to an essential aspect of manhood—his noble appearance, his solitariness, his sense of duty, his seriousness and depth:

> This Ushant, in all weathers, was ever alert at his duty; intrepidly mounting the fore-yard in a gale, his long beard streaming like Neptune's. Off Cape Horn it looked like a miller's, being all over powdered with frost: sometimes it glittered with minute icicles in the pale, cold, moonlit Patagonian nights. But though he was so active in time of tempest, yet when his duty did not call for exertion, he was a remarkably staid, reserved, silent, and majestic old man, holding himself aloof from noisy revelry, and never participating in the boisterous sports of the crew. He resolutely set his beard against their boyish frolickings. . . . (p. 353)

Of even greater significance than his appearance and manner, however, is Ushant's continual questing after the meaning of life. No man could be truly noble in Melville's eyes unless he was a questioner:

> Nor was his philosophy to be despised; it abounded in wisdom. For this Ushant was an old man, of strong natural sense, who had seen nearly the whole terraqueous globe, and could reason of civilized and savage, of Gentile and Jew, of Christian and Moslem. . . . I never could look at him, and survey his right reverend beard,

75

without bestowing upon him that title which, in one of his satires, Persius gives to the immortal quaffer of the hemlock—*Magister Barbatus*—the bearded master. (p. 353)

Ushant, then, is White-Jacket's idol of manhood, his teacher in the meaning of true dignity. For Ushant, as for White-Jacket, the voyage of the *Neversink* is a trial because the captain attempts to deprive him of his manhood. Ushant sees his beard as so much a part of himself that a shave would be emasculation. White-Jacket realizes the symbolic value of the beard and sees the height of nobility even an old man can reach. Although Ushant is flogged and imprisoned when he refuses to cut his beard, in the end he is victorious. He reaches home with his beard and his dignity. Significantly the chapters involving Ushant's crisis over his beard come near the end of the book when White-Jacket loses his jacket. What he has learned from Ushant constitutes the final stage of his growth to manhood. After that he falls and cuts away the garment of youth.

Doubles, the jacket, disguises, and beards—all are symbols and metaphors of the central and complex idea of amputation. Often the process of separating or cutting away is necessary to reach manhood. In other cases, with Ushant's beard, for example, severance would result in a loss of it. Whatever the case, amputation is of primary importance, and its recurrence in several forms gives the book coherence. White-Jacket's final separation from his jacket is the dramatic culmination of a pattern that builds throughout the narrative. References to amputation occur many times. Off Cape Horn the weather was so cold "any man could have undergone amputation with great ease, and helped take up the arteries himself" (p. 101). One reference to amputation prepares for another, and when the next one appears, it points up—sometimes with poignant irony—the difference in context and implication between the two references. The result is a kind of rhythm which unifies the book and underscores the theme. When Cuticle amputates a crewman's leg in Chapter 63, his question to a fellow surgeon echoes the earlier comment on amputation: " 'Surgeon Sawyer,' now said Cuticle, courteously turning to the surgeon of the *Buccaneer*, 'would you like to take up the arteries?' " (p. 262). The variations, however, make this pattern of repetition effective. When Cuticle operates, the weather is not cold, but hot; the patient does not undergo the amputation "with great ease," but with the greatest possible anguish, both physical and mental; and finally, the poor crewman does not help "take up the arteries himself"—is not, that is, the master of his own fate—but is deprived of his manhood and, indeed, of his life by a scrawny and aged surgeon who is but a shadow of a man.

This amputation scene prepares for another of a very different kind—the amputation of the beards in Chapter 84. The operating facilities in Chapter 63 consist of, among other things, "two match-tubs, near by, placed one upon another," and various cutting implements in full view. The crudeness of this arrangement is recalled by the barber's facilities in the later chapter, which are described in similar terms with the customer as amputee. The barber's furniture "merely consisted of a match-tub, elevated upon a shot-box, as a barber's chair for the patient" (p. 351). Similarly the crude razors remind us of the surgeon's tools. In both instances something is to be amputated: in the earlier chapter a man's leg is cut off by a surgeon who is no man; in the later chapter the symbols of manhood, beards, are ordered removed by a captain who is at best half a man. The soulless are ever eager to cut away whatever lends dignity and independence to another.

The operation scene in Chapter 63 also prepares for still another amputation, which, unlike Cuticle's needless butchery, is necessary. With satanic irony Cuticle feels the edge of his knife and remarks: "Yes . . . amputation is our only resource" (p. 256). It is far from the only resource in that situation, but the greater irony is that in White-Jacket's case Cuticle's remark is accurate. He must amputate what has come to seem a part of himself, the white jacket; and while the operation will not be painless, it is essential.

The imagery of that celebrated scene in Chapter 92, where White-Jacket plunges from aloft into the sea, comes up, and tears himself free from his coat, has frequently been interpreted in terms of death and rebirth—a baptism into new life. There are suggestions of birth in White-Jacket's description, but imagery of a man giving birth to himself also presents some obvious problems. White-Jacket's struggle with his jacket seems more in keeping with the pattern of amputation which runs throughout the book: "I strove to tear it off; but it was looped together here and there, and the strings were not then to be sundered by hand. I whipped out my knife, that was tucked at my belt, and ripped my jacket straight up and down, as if I were ripping open myself. With a violent struggle I then burst out of it, and was free. Heavily soaked, it slowly sank before my eyes" (p. 394). Pointing toward this scene are all previous references to amputation. White-Jacket has become that "man" mentioned in Chapter 25, who has "undergone amputation, and helped take up the arteries himself."

All forms of amputation in *White-Jacket* do not mean the same thing; some are necessary and ennobling, others destructive and degrading. Ushant's beard means everything to him, and if he had followed Claret's order and had it cut, he would have severed his manhood. On the other hand, Jack Chase, White-Jacket's other "sea tutor," allows his own beard to be removed without a loss of dignity. Indeed, with Chase as with White-Jacket, amputation is symbolically the *means* of acquiring manhood rather than a threat to it, for in the process of acquiring manhood, Chase has lost a finger. White-Jacket, like his model in manhood, becomes an amputee in becoming a man.

OMOO: Trial by Pleasure

Chapter 5

Omoo: *A Narrative of Adventures in the South Seas* presents its hero in an interlude of pleasure between the adversity of Tommo and the futile and half-wild wanderings of Taji in *Mardi*, Melville's next book. Resembling the heroes of a picaresque novel, the narrator and his companion, Long Ghost, take part in a bloodless mutiny and then wander from place to place on Tahiti and Imeeo, never allowing the burden of worry to weigh on them heavily or long.

Although the temptation to think of *Omoo* as merely a sequel to *Typee* is strong, the two books are vastly different.[1] *Omoo*, it seems

1. The tendency to link *Typee* and *Omoo* began almost with their publication. Gordon Roper accurately described the situation: "These two books, the first of Melville's literary children, became the Siamese twins of the literary world for most of his nineteenth-century readers" ("Historical Note" to *Omoo*, Northwestern-Newberry Edition, 1968, p. 319). The trend to think of the two books collectively continued into the twentieth century as evidenced by the fact that several critical studies of Melville's work group the two books into the same chapter. The view of James E. Miller, Jr., is representative of many: "*Typee* and *Omoo* should be read as one continuous work just as they recount one continuous adventure. Moreover, the informing

to me, is no more a continuation of *Typee* than, say, *Huckleberry Finn* is of *Tom Sawyer*. In both cases the authors simply began their new books where the old ones ended. Melville himself made this point in his Preface: "The present narrative necessarily begins where 'Typee' concludes, but has no further connection with the latter work. All, therefore, necessary for the reader to understand, who has not read 'Typee,' is given in a brief introduction" (p. xiv). In a letter to his English publisher, John Murray, Melville introduced his new book as "of a totally different character from 'Typee.' "[2]

The differences are many and deep, but the most apparent is in the two narrators.[3] The hero of *Typee* had a very bad time of it. The narrator of *Omoo* is disturbed at much he sees, but he does not suffer; indeed, he frequently enjoys himself—a rare situation for one of Melville's heroes. He does not experience that brooding anxiety that plagues Tommo. No suspense is created over his fate; he is not threatened by cannibalism, mysterious taboos, or ill-health. He has no illusions about recapturing the past. Like all Melville's heroes he is restless and dissatisfied, but he does not attempt to go back and regain some past happiness. Whereas in *Typee* Melville suggested the difference between Tommo's past and present states of mind by contrasting his previous feelings about Typee with those of the moment, no such distinction is noticeable in *Omoo*. The past and present seem one.

---

sensibility in each is identical, and the serious thematic content does not alter. . . . In other words, *Typee* and *Omoo* form one continuous picaresque tale which is divided merely for the sake of convenience into two volumes" (*A Reader's Guide to Herman Melville*, New York, 1962, p. 21).

2. *The Letters of Herman Melville*, ed. Merrell R. Davis and William H. Gilman (New Haven, 1960), p. 41.

3. In *Herman Melville: The Tragedy of Mind* (Cambridge, Mass., 1944), William Ellery Sedgwick comments perceptively on another aspect of this difference: "In spite of the external continuity between them, *Omoo* is entirely different in internal atmosphere from its predecessor. Without the poetry of *Typee*, it has far more humor. It is the least moody of all Melville's books" (p. 36).

In fact, the narrator of *Omoo* resembles White-Jacket (after he reaches manhood) a great deal more than he does Tommo. Furthermore, the central subject of *Omoo* is closely related to that of *White-Jacket*. The independence which the hero of *White-Jacket* painfully acquires is put to the test in *Omoo*. It is, in Melville's work, a peculiar test, for the challenge comes not in the guise of pain but pleasure. *Omoo* is thus the portrayal of a hero in somewhat unheroic conditions. He makes no Promethean attempts to do the impossible. Nevertheless, his independence, which is to say his individuality as a thinking and questioning human being, his very inner life, is threatened throughout by two perniciously subtle forces—pleasurable indolence and a potentially destructive friendship.

Perhaps the clearest way of showing how this trial by pleasure functions is to compare it with a situation in another work where essentially the same thing takes place, Shakespeare's *Henry IV, Part I*. The unmistakable hero of the play is Prince Hal (not Falstaff or Hotspur).[4] Falstaff is there, among other reasons, to present a challenge, a test, to a young man soon to be king. It could be called the test of the Boar's Head Tavern. It is one thing to show courage in the face of obvious danger—Hal has ample time to do that in battle—but something else to be taken into the company of an irresistible rogue and his group of reprobates, to live among them enjoying their pleasures and thus appearing to be one of them, and yet to retain one's princely identity even in the face of a blackened reputation.

Hal does just that and prepares the way for his great heroism on the field of battle in the last act and for his ultimate success as a model king in *Henry IV, Part II*. What M. A. Shaaber writes about Prince Hal expresses much that is true about the narrator of *Omoo*: "The prince really does little or nothing reprehensible: he takes part in the robbery, but his character is carefully safeguarded from the start and he restores the money with advantage;

4. See, for example, J. Dover Wilson, *The Fortunes of Falstaff* (Cambridge, 1944).

otherwise he only gets a little tipsy . . . and exchanges vituperation with Falstaff. It is Falstaff who creates the atmosphere of depravity, the prince sharing in it but not responsible for it and always standing somewhat apart from it."[5] The Prince's rejection of Falstaff is neither cruel nor unexpected. Hal is never anything but a true prince. To Shakespeare's audience he would be seen as a greater man because he could live with the delightful but corrupt Falstaff without himself becoming tainted. The model king remains aloof and inviolable even while seemingly enjoying himself in the lowest company. To pass successfully through the trial of pleasure is extremely difficult because it is a test without pain or pressure. Yet many a man wakes up after an interlude of pleasure to discover he has become incurably like those he did not want to join. The narrator of *Omoo* is Melville's Prince Hal, Tahiti and Imeeo his Boar's Head, and Long Ghost his Falstaff (albeit a skinny one). Like Prince Hal he enjoys a kind of saturnalian holiday. But as C. L. Barber has pointed out in his discussion of *Henry IV*, the purpose of traditional saturnalian ritual was not permanent escape from responsibility but clarification, a fresh start, through release.[6] *Omoo* fits squarely into this ancient tradition, and Long Ghost is, like Falstaff, a splendid personification of Misrule.

Readers have generally been much too kind to Long Ghost.[7]

5. Introduction to *The First Part of King Henry the Fourth* (Baltimore, 1957), p. 22. C. L. Barber observes that "the prince's sports, accordingly, express not dissoluteness but a fine excess of vitality . . . together with a capacity for occasionally looking at the world as though it were upside down. His energy is controlled by an inclusive awareness of the rhythm in which he is living: despite appearances, he will not make the mistake which undid Richard II, who played at saturnalia until it caught up with him in earnest." See "From Ritual to Comedy: An Examination of *Henry IV*," in *English Stage Comedy*, ed. W. K. Wimsatt, Jr., *English Institute Essays*, 1954 (New York, 1955), p. 29.

6. Barber, p. 25.

7. He delighted D. H. Lawrence (as did the whole book). See *Studies in Classic American Literature* (Garden City, N. Y., 1955), pp. 152–54. Lewis Mumford thought him "a capital fellow" and saw him as so like the narrator that they come together "as naturally as one globule of mercury will coalesce

Few critics have seen him in an unfavorable light.[8] Yet he represents all that is inimical to Melville's hero. Throughout his close association with Long Ghost the narrator is on trial, but there is as little chance that he will adopt the doctor's ways and attitudes as there is in *Henry IV, Part I* that Hal will join Falstaff's gang permanently and abdicate his role as prince and king. The narrator and Hal are both tried by their pleasant associations with wags, but the outcome is not really in question. Nevertheless, their virtues are made clearer because of the challenge.

Long Ghost's role in *Omoo* resembles that of Falstaff in several ways. He is full of good humor and comic pretentiousness. Although he is skinny, he eats with a vigor worthy of Falstaff: "Others occasionally went about seeking what they might devour, but *he* was always on the alert" (p. 132). In fact, he is almost entirely motivated by one appetite or another. He seems to live, as Falstaff does, for the satisfaction of his physical cravings. When he is called upon to work for Zeke and Shorty, he reveals a comical

---

with another as soon as they touch" (*Herman Melville*, New York, 1929, p. 33). Charles R. Anderson in *Melville in the South Seas* (New York, 1939) went so far as to call him "Melville's hero 'Long Ghost,'" and "this picaresque hero of *Omoo* to whom Melville played both Boswell and Sancho Panza" (p. 203). Newton Arvin referred to him as "the real protagonist of *Omoo*" (*Herman Melville*, New York, 1950, p. 86). And F. O. Matthiessen believed that "the kind of life he [Melville] relishes is epitomized in the portrait of Dr. Long Ghost in *Omoo*" (*American Renaissance*, New York, 1941, p. 378).

8. Ronald Mason, in *The Spirit Above the Dust* (London, 1951), objected to the high praise usually paid Long Ghost, but his objection was based on what he considered Melville's failure to characterize effectively. He found him "merely a static portrait of eccentricity" (p. 43). Edwin M. Eigner, "The Romantic Unity of Melville's *Omoo*," *Philological Quarterly*, XLVI (1967), seems closest to the truth when he calls Long Ghost, "the kind of man the narrator is in danger of becoming" (p. 98). I agree with Eigner's implication that the two are different but not with the notion that the narrator is in danger of becoming another Long Ghost. Newton Arvin makes a point similar to Eigner's when he states that Long Ghost "embodies the complete footlooseness, the perfect irresponsibility, which Melville, on one side of his nature, would have liked to attain" (p. 86).

aversion to labor or, indeed, to any form of physical exertion.[9] He shows a Falstaffian physical ineptness in a bullock hunt:

> The action over, the heavy artillery came up, in the person of the Long Doctor, with his blunderbuss.
> "Where are they?" he cried, out of breath.
> "A mile or two h'off, by this time," replied the Cockney. (p. 219)

The doctor's high flown rhetoric and exaggerated gentlemanly manners add a great deal to the comic tone of *Omoo*. He introduces the narrator to a native in this manner: " 'Permit me, my dear Darby, to introduce to you my esteemed friend and comrade, Paul,' said the doctor, gallanting me up with all the grimace and flourish imaginable" (p. 254).

Like Falstaff, Long Ghost thus has an attractiveness which has won the heart and distorted the vision of many a reader. He is witty, charming, and carefree. Members of the crew find themselves intimidated by his education and flattered by his voluntary association with them. He is no snob, though he seems high born. Little wonder, then, that the narrator chose such a companion for his wanderings.

Despite his appeal, however, Long Ghost has practically nothing in common with the narrator. Even before they leave for Imeeo, the narrator confesses, "I somewhat distrusted the doctor, for he was no sailor . . ." (p. 160). The fundamental difference between the two characters is symbolically shown when they go on a secretive expedition for food to a ship in the harbor one night: "Assuming the command of the expedition, upon the strength of my being a sailor, I packed the Long Doctor with a paddle in the bow, and then shoving off, leaped into the stern; thus leaving him to do all the work, and reserving to myself the dignified sinecure of steering. All would have gone well, were it not that my paddler made such clumsy work that the water spattered, and showered

---

9. The narrator, on the other hand, shows no constitutional objection to work but merely to this particular form of it.

down upon us without ceasing" (pp. 160–61). Long Ghost is such a poor seaman that he turns over the canoe. The narrator then discovers that the doctor cannot even swim.[10]

Long Ghost's lack of skill as a sailor is suggestive (as I will later show) of his lack of fundamental virtues. He is such a delightful companion that the reader sometimes has to remind himself that Long Ghost is depraved. A partial list of his characteristics would have to include hypocrisy, cowardice, dishonesty, laziness, gluttony, and lustfulness. He is a liar, an imbiber of laudanum, and a rake. Although he finds Long Ghost amusing and develops a certain affection for him, the narrator never indicates that he respects him. He sees through Long Ghost as few others do, and when the doctor becomes too obnoxious, as he does at Zeke and Shorty's, the narrator's affection fades quickly: "Nor did the humorous doctor forbear to foster an opinion every way so advantageous to himself; at times, for the sake of a joke, assuming airs of superiority over myself, which, though laughable enough, were sometimes annoying" (p. 231). He can laugh at Long Ghost and enjoy his intelligence and wit, but he never gets his values mixed up; he never mistakes Long Ghost for anything more than he is—an amiable landsman who can never know or share his own values. When he senses that his own identity or integrity is being challenged, he quickly responds. At one point he writes: "To tell the plain truth, things at last came to such a pass, that I told him, up and down, that I had no notion to put up with his pretentions" (p. 231).

This fundamental difference between the narrator and Long Ghost is seen clearest in the closing pages when the interlude on the land is drawing to a close and when the narrator feels strongly the need to get back to sea. Much earlier he hints at his restlessness to return to sea: he indicates that he wanted to go to Taloo partly

10. On p. 161 Melville writes of Long Ghost: "But the secret was, he was unable to swim. . . ." He seems to have forgotten this detail by p. 252, however, when he states: "The doctor was in famous spirits; removing his Roora, he went splashing into the sea; and, after swimming a few yards, waded ashore. . . ."

because "of the facilities presented [there] for going to sea in the whaler . . ." (p. 246). Toward the end he writes: "Weary somewhat of life in Imeeo, like all sailors ashore, I at last pined for the billows" (p. 312). When he tries to convince the captain of the *Leviathan* to sign on Long Ghost, the captain instinctively reacts with abhorrence: "It was evident that he took Long Ghost for an exceedingly problematical character" (p. 314), and he is adamant. He recognizes the narrator for a true sailor, but he sees in Long Ghost none of the qualities he wants in a seaman.

With the captain's decision the hero has passed the final test. He has come to the end of his wanderings on land; he has lived with a landsman, but, as the captain's judgment significantly suggests, he has not changed. Although he leaves the carefree Long Ghost reluctantly, there could be no other course open to him.[11] Long Ghost realizes the gulf between them: "As for himself, on second thoughts, he was no sailor; and although 'landsmen' very often compose part of a whaler's crew, he did not quite relish the idea of occupying a position so humble" (p. 315). Only momentarily does the narrator consider remaining: "I turned the matter over; and at last decided upon quitting the island. The impulse urging me to sea once more . . . [was] too much to be resisted" (p. 315). For a while he had left the open sea for a kind of Boar's Head interlude of pleasure and carefree living with a Falstaffian companion, but at the end he is compelled by what he is to return to the "open independence of . . . sea."

In *Omoo* as in *Henry IV* friendship is therefore valued less highly than fidelity to self. Both Prince Hal and Melville's hero have a greater commitment to their sense of personal identity than to their friends. The subject of friendship is frequently discussed throughout *Omoo*. The narrator relates in a number of places how friendship has eroded in Tahiti. The Tahitians at one time may have been genuine in their expressions of friendship, but that day is past. Now they use friendship for material ends, and their

11. For an opposing view on the appropriateness of the ending, see Eigner, p. 106.

gestures are hollow. He tells of an islander named Kooloo who approached him with numerous expressions of admiration and esteem. After receiving gifts, however, Kooloo carried his friendship to greener fields. Most of the sailors encounter in the natives the same gross materialism clothed in a garb of friendship.

In the paragraph preceding his account of Kooloo, the narrator speaks of his friend, Long Ghost. The label is ironic, for Long Ghost is no more a deep and abiding friend than is Kooloo. In fact, the point seems to be that friendship is largely an illusory conception. Men feel it temporarily in moments of one kind of intoxication or another. The comic scene where Long Ghost and Varvy (the native with his own whiskey still) get drunk together suggests the transiency of friendship:

> Every one knows that, so long as the occasion lasts, there is no stronger bond of sympathy and good-feeling among men, than getting tipsy together. And how earnestly, nay, movingly, a brace of worthies, thus employed, will endeavor to shed light upon, and elucidate their mystical ideas!
>
> Fancy Varvy and the doctor, then; lovingly tippling, and brimming over with a desire to become better acquainted; the doctor politely bent upon carrying on the conversation in the language of his host, and the old hermit persisting in trying to talk English. The result was, that between the two, they made such a fricassee of vowels and consonants, that it was enough to turn one's brain. (p. 274)

The next morning Long Ghost leaves, bitterly accusing Varvy of being a thief.

If friendship is an illusion, then what remains? Melville's answer rings throughout his works—independence. Men like the narrator recognize the basic virtues in others—White-Jacket can thus admire Jack Chase and Ishmael, Queequeg—but that does not alter the fact that they are ultimately alone, an isolated self behind the insuperable wall of flesh, blood, and bone. They may suffer from the loneliness, but they know they must live within themselves; reality—or at least all that can be known of reality—comes from within. So they cherish their independence. Not even so amiable a fellow as Long Ghost in so pleasurable a place as Tahiti can intrude upon that independence or alter the sense of identity which a man like the narrator of *Omoo* possesses.

When his call comes Prince Hal goes back to the royal fold, which seems a far different thing from merely returning to sea in a whaler. But actually it is not. In both cases the important factor is the denouncing of a temporary life of aimlessness and irresponsibility in order to take up one's proper work—whether it be as a king or as a seaman is of secondary importance.

Here we reach the heart of *Omoo*. The narrator is almost constantly concerned with the idea of work. While he is describing the pleasant, leisurely way of life in Tahiti, another voice, a deeper and quieter and more sombre one, is heard whispering, "The horror! The horror!" He refers time and again to the natives' aversion to any kind of labor. "In Tahiti," he remarks, "the people have nothing to do; and idleness, everywhere, is the parent of vice" (p. 190). He gives numerous examples of the islanders' failure to stick to any kind of sustained work. When the cultivation of cotton was first tried on Tahiti, the natives "with their usual love of novelty . . . went to work with great alacrity; but the interest excited quickly subsided, and now, not a pound of the article is raised" (p. 190). The island depends largely upon breadfruit trees for food, yet the Tahitians will not even take the little trouble to plant them. At one time some eager industrialist thought he could introduce weaving there and sent out machinery from London: "The whiz of the wheels and spindles brought in volunteers from all quarters, who deemed it a privilege to be admitted to work: yet, in six months, not a boy could be hired; and the machinery was knocked down, and packed off to Sydney" (p. 190). When sugar plantations were started, the same pattern repeated itself.

For some of the laziness (and much of the vice) among Tahitians, the narrator blames European intruders, including missionaries, who made the natives give up their old ways for new ones that they could not assimilate. Nevertheless, it is clear that despite all the evils which civilization has brought to the innocent natives, the basic problem to the narrator's mind is that the Tahitian seems by nature to lack depth. And the evidence for this conclusion is that the natives do not have and never had, even before the coming of Captain Cook, the slightest propensity for *work*.[12] As long as there was little disease and none of the sophisticated corruption of the civilized world to prey upon them, they could live blissful lives, but when evil came, they had no protection because beneath the innocence there was no individuality, no inner life. The narrator is appalled at missionaries not because he believes they are evil but because he thinks most of them are stupid. They should have known when to leave well enough alone. Instead they tried naively to give the islanders a new identity through work—for true Christianity is just as surely a form of work as physical labor. At first the Tahitians seemed to embrace the new religion. Thousands were "saved" almost immediately upon the arrival of the missionaries. They professed belief, took the new names which the missionaries gave them, and with some reluctance even changed their everyday way of life in accordance with their new-found morality. It took them about as long to give up spiritual labor for Christ as it did to abandon the task of weaving or the cultivation of sugar cane.[13]

The narrator does not hold the Tahitians responsible for their physical and spiritual indolence. He would not try to make them into anything other than what they are by nature—a happy, lazy, innocent people—because he assumes that such an attempt would be clearly futile. He is angered by those who refuse to recognize that fact. Blameless though they are, the Tahitians nevertheless disturb him.

12. One exception is the people of Tamai, where the narrator and Long Ghost see "the manufacture of tappa . . . going on in several buildings" (p. 239).

13. Po-Po, the narrator and Long Ghost's kind host in Partoowye, is a notable exception: "But whatever others might have been, Po-Po was, in truth, a Christian: the only one, Arfretee [Po-Po's wife] excepted, whom I personally knew to be such, among all the natives of Polynesia" (p. 280).

He is bothered by the infectiousness of Tahitian indolence, which presents an even greater challenge to his independence than Long Ghost. What he observes when late in the book he and Long Ghost manage to invade the "palace" of the native queen illustrates this point. Inside the royal abode the narrator experiences sensations of strangeness and surprise when he sees fine products of the labors of civilized man cast about the room casually without any apparent order or awareness of what they represent:

> Cheek by jowl, they lay beside the rudest native articles, without the slightest attempt at order. Superb writing-desks of rosewood, inlaid with silver and mother-of-pearl; decanters and goblets of cut glass; embossed volumes of plates; gilded candelabras; sets of globes and mathematical instruments; the finest porcelain; richly mounted sabres and fowling-pieces; laced hats and sumptuous garments of all sorts, with numerous other matters of European manufacture, were strewn about among greasy calabashes half-filled with *"poee."* (pp. 309–10)

Even more significant than the juxtaposition of these emblems of civilized labor with those of native sloth is the narrator's implication that the Tahitian way of life engulfs and finally destroys all evidences of civilized endeavor: all these beautiful and useful items of European origins in the queen's palace are damaged—"the fowling-pieces and swords were rusted; the finest woods were scratched; and a folio volume of Hogarth lay open, with a cocoa-nut shell of some musty preparation capsized" on it (p. 310). On another occasion the narrator describes a group of houses erected by an enterprising American carpenter. It was an entire block of "regular square frames, boarded over, furnished with windows and doorways, and two stories high." They were "fast going to decay," however, all of them having "settled down nearly a foot" (p. 285). Except for a few Gypsies and "vagabond natives," no one used these dwellings of civilization.

Men can rust in Tahiti as readily as fine swords or decay as quickly as houses, and once the process begins, it is inexorable. One of the native diseases of Tahiti and neighboring islands is the "Fa-Fa," which "seems to have prevailed among them from the earliest antiquity" (p. 127). This disease is highly suggestive of a deeper affliction of the soul. It causes no pain and does not interfere with a life of cheerfulness. It is "very gradual in its approaches," but it is incurable. White men are thought to be immune to it, but they are not, as the narrator proves in describing a certain sailor whom he had seen on the island of Roorooto, a short distance from Tahiti: "His hair and beard were unshorn, his face deadly pale and haggard, and one limb swelled with the Fa-Fa to an incredible bigness" (p. 128). This man, who has been on the island for years, has taken up native ways and native attitudes; he has given up working. The psychological effects of "going native" are symbolized by his physical disease. Coming upon him gradually, the malady follows its steady course to the victim's destruction. It marks him as a doomed man to the outside world, and when he wishes to escape, no sea captain will agree to take him on board. All civilized men are marked who try to live the life of Tahiti.

The most striking example of such a man—Melville called his type the "renegado"—is Lem Hardy, an Englishman who had deserted his ship ten years before and had immediately become a leader among the natives. He was a "renegado from Christendom and *humanity*—a white man, in the South Sea girdle, and tattooed in the face" (p. 27, italics mine). The tattoo seems even more terrible to the narrator than the Fa-Fa, for the diseased sailor wished to escape but could not, whereas Lem Hardy has no desire to return. He had "thrown it up forever"; the struggle to find his place in the civilized world was too difficult, and he has thus given up his "humanity" with the abandon of Conrad's Kurtz. That he found no less a heart of darkness is shown by the tattoo, "a broad blue band [which] stretched across his face from ear to ear" and "the taper figure of a blue shark" on his forehead. "Some of us," continues Melville, "gazed upon this man with a feeling akin to horror, no ways abated when informed that he had voluntarily submitted to this embellishment of his countenance. What an impress! Far worse than Cain's—*his* was perhaps a wrinkle, or a freckle, which some of our modern cosmetics might have effaced; but the blue shark was a mark indelible, which all the waters of Abana and Pharpar, rivers of Damascus, could never wash out" (p. 27). Melville's Biblical reference is to a Syrian, Naaman, who suffered from leprosy and who realized that the two principal rivers of his country could not cure him.[14] Lem Hardy, too, suffers from an incurable disease, which like the Fa-Fa is subtle in its early stages without pain or discomfort but in the end fatal to his "humanity."

Such warnings about the moral and psychological dangers of a life without work—the furnishings of the queen's palace, sunken and decayed houses, a diseased white sailor, a tattooed renegado —are sprinkled throughout *Omoo*. The narrator goes to Tahiti, experiences its beauty and appeal, recognizes also its dangers, and in the end escapes. Within this framework, the basic pattern is repeated in individual sections of the book. Chapters 63, 64, and 65, for example, form a unit of structure which repeats the overall pattern. These three chapters describe the experiences of the narrator and Long Ghost in the inland village of Tamai. They watch an ancient dance, the "Lory-Lory," and are much taken with the primitive abandon of the native girls; the narrator has a puzzling experience with an old native, who tries to sell him a pair of pants; the narrator and Long Ghost are informed of some natives who have come to Tamai looking for runaway sailors; they escape and return to the plantation of Zeke and Shorty. Like most of *Omoo* these episodes are deceptive in their seeming casualness. *Omoo* has so often been described as Melville's most autobiographical and factual novel (and therefore the least inventive and artistic),[15] that

14. See 2 Kings 5:12.

15. Charles R. Anderson discussed Melville's indebtedness to sources, but he concluded that most of the adventures in *Omoo* "were drawn almost literally from actual experience." He designated it as "perhaps the most strictly autobiographical of all Melville's works" (p. 199). That tag stuck. Eigner's recent article states categorically that Melville's biographers find it the "most veracious autobiography of all Melville's South Sea volumes,"

these incidents might be taken as aimless but entertaining—a little exotic romance and local color, a bit of humor, and a dash of light adventure. These chapters deserve close attention, however, because through them the seriousness of *Omoo* as a genuine work of art can perhaps be suggested.

The three chapters present an intensification of the narrator's overall Tahitian experience of appeal-warning-escape. At no other time does the native way of life seem so alluring as in Tamai. All the charms of Tahiti and Imeeo seem concentrated in this village, where many of the old ways persist and where civilization has least intruded. It is a distilled Tahiti—100 proof. The height of its

---

quoting Anderson (p. 95). The persistence with which *Omoo* continues to be regarded by some readers as non-fiction is all the more puzzling in the face of such biographers and critics as Leon Howard and Gordon Roper, who have both written correctives to Anderson's over-emphasis on the autobiographical element in *Omoo*. After a careful examination of contemporary documents dealing with the *Lucy Ann* mutiny (documents which did not come to light until after Anderson's *Melville in the South Seas*, 1939—see Roper, p. 343), Howard wrote a concise and accurate statement of his findings, which threw new light on Melville's inventiveness in *Omoo*: "The greater part of *Omoo* was neither exactly fact nor pure invention: it was a convincing narrative of what might have been had the runaway Melville been a little more bold and a little more carefree than he actually was. If he had been more active in the mutiny on board the *Lucy Ann*, he might have played the role he attributed to himself on the *Julia* and, consequently, really would have been sent in irons aboard *La Reine Blanche* and kept in the native calaboose as long as he indicated. Or, if he had stayed for two months instead of two weeks on the island of Eimeo, he could have had experiences very much like those he described" (*Herman Melville*, Berkeley, 1951, pp. 100–101). Actually *Omoo* is probably no less a product of Melville's imagination than *Typee*. He changed big facts and small ones, altered time, and changed the sequence of events that he had experienced. As Gordon Roper has stated: "Melville altered important facts of the actual history partly because he did not know the full story and partly because some of what he did know had undergone change in his memory; but probably he made his major alterations to gain dramatic effect" (p. 321). In addition Melville departed frequently and extensively from his own experience to borrow whole chunks of material about Polynesia from such books as William Ellis's *Polynesian Researches* (1833). With effective irony Leon Howard has charged that "without the unconscious help of the missionary, William Ellis, *Omoo* might never have been finished" (p. 101).

appeal is seen in the Lory-Lory. Significantly the narrator and Long Ghost have to be covered by robes of tappa and their faces hooded in order to attend the dance.[16] Throughout *Omoo* clothing is symbolic; the robes of tappa here suggest another set of values which have to be assumed (in this case it is only temporarily) to enjoy what the islands have to offer. Chapter 63, therefore, is a treatment in miniature and in much greater intensity of the general appeal of Tahiti found throughout the book and with the suggestion often repeated elsewhere that civilized man must surrender his own identity in order to embrace the Tahitian way.

Chapter 63 presents the appeal; Chapter 64, the warning. It suggests what happens when civilized man abandons his own garments too long for those of Tahiti. In this episode another side of Tamai is seen; it is represented not by its beautiful maidens in dance but by an old native man "of a most hideous aspect" who lives in a "mere kennel" of a hut on the outskirts of the village (p. 243). This frightful old "goblin" entices the narrator to his dwelling apparently for the purpose of showing him something: "At last, he clutched a calabash, stained black, and with the neck broken off; on one side of it was a large hole. Something seemed to be stuffed away in the vessel; and after a deal of poking at the aperture, a musty old pair of sailor trowsers was drawn forth" (p. 244). He offers to sell the trousers, but the narrator, badly shaken, runs out and does not stop until he reaches the village. The shadowy figure of that unknown sailor looms large here. What was he doing in Tamai? How did the old native come to acquire his garment? What became of him? All that is left is the piece of clothing, the symbol of his calling, stuffed into a dirty calabash and now too moldy to be of use. Judging from the narrator's actions, he subconsciously recognizes the implications just as he does elsewhere with other warnings. This, however, is an intensified warning just as the dance in the previous chapter is an intensified appeal. The only other time in which the narrator experiences such

16. Even in Tamai, however, and with the taking on of symbolic robes, the narrator is never deeply tempted.

94

revulsion is when he looks upon Lem Hardy. There is further significance in the fact that Long Ghost refuses to go with "the old clothsman" and in that the narrator never reveals what he saw to the doctor. Here, as throughout the book, Long Ghost refuses to see warnings and remains forever in the dark.

Escape in Chapter 65 is also intensified, for unlike other places —escape from the *Julia*, from the calabooza, from Zeke and Shorty's plantation, and the narrator's escape from the island at the end— there is here grave and immediate danger. The appeal and consequently the danger represented by Tamai are magnified; therefore, the escape should be dramatic. "Plunging into the groves," the narrator writes, "we thanked our stars that we had thus narrowly escaped being apprehended as runaway seamen, and marched off the beach. *This, at least, was what we thought we had escaped*" (p. 246, italics mine). They had, of course, escaped much more.

As an analysis of Chapters 63–65 reveals, *Omoo* is as symbolic as it is literal. Tahiti is a concept as well as an actual place. And on the symbolic level Tahiti suggests at least three different meanings. The first is the Tahiti of prelapsarian man, a beautiful and peaceful garden surrounded by the pain and uncertainties unknown as yet to unfallen Adam. In this sense Tahiti represents the state of innocence. On the second level it is fallen man's *memory* of innocence. Ishmael, himself scarred by knowledge and painful experience, uses Tahiti to suggest the remembered state of innocence when he says in *Moby-Dick*:

> Consider all this; and then turn to this green, gentle, and most docile earth; consider them both, the sea and the land; and do you not find a strange analogy to something in yourself? For as this appalling ocean surrounds the verdant land, so in the soul of man there lies one insular Tahiti, full of peace and joy, but encompassed by all the horrors of the half known life.[17]

17. *Moby-Dick*, ed. Harrison Hayford and Hershel Parker (New York, 1967), p. 236.

As most of Melville's work makes clear, one can remember that "one insular Tahiti," but cannot actually return to it. "God keep thee," continues Ishmael, now addressing not those like himself who can only remember Tahiti but those who still dwell there, "push not off from that isle, thou canst never return." If man insists upon trying to go back, he will but land upon the degrading lee shore, Melville's third Tahiti. All three levels of meaning are associated with Tahiti in *Omoo*, frequently at the same time, making it a rich and suggestive symbol. But Ishmael's statement needs one further comment for clarification. His advice never to push off in the first place resembles that of an adult who writes in a child's school annual or autograph book, "Stay as you are." And actually the situations are not dissimilar. Ishmael has seen too much of life and at the moment he makes that statement he yearns for a previous time of innocence, just as an adult remembers his childhood. Yet the adult knows very well that children must (and should) change, and Ishmael fully recognizes the ennoblement of the fortunate fall; he knows that it is in the howling infinite that one's humanity is felt, not on the comfortable shore of that "one insular Tahiti."

In whatever sense Tahiti is used in *Omoo*, it is always a threat to personal independence because there can be no independence without work. Now it should be made clear that work for Melville was not simply physical labor. In *Omoo* work is a metaphor for that activity, whatever it may be, which most nearly frees a man. Marlowe's comment on work in Conrad's "Heart of Darkness" comes very near to expressing what Melville was getting at in *Omoo*: "No, I don't like work. I had rather laze about and think of all the fine things that can be done. I don't like work—no man does—but I like what is in the work,—the chance to find yourself. Your own reality—for yourself, not for others—what no other man can ever know. They can only see the mere show, and never can tell what it really means."[18]

18. *Youth and Two Other Stories, Complete Works of Joseph Conrad*, Kent edition (New York, 1925), XVI, 85. Conrad's world view is probably

Working, in this sense, presupposes there is substance in the man, that there is some reality to be found. That being the case, some men have no proper[19] work because they are hopelessly without identity. Such men are either totally inept in whatever jobs they are doing, or they seem to be vocational dilettantes, superficially clever in doing many things but truly skillful never and profoundly committed to none. Melville deeply respects the man who knows his job and performs it well. In *Redburn* he wrote: "To distinguish such a mariner from those who merely '*hand, reef, and steer*,' that is, run aloft, furl sails, haul ropes, and stand at the wheel, they say he is '*a sailor-man*;' which means that he not only knows how to reef a topsail, but is an artist in the rigging" (p. 121). In the next century Ernest Hemingway was to use the same metaphor of work to portray the "code hero," the man who has found his own reality, who has torn from the chaos of life dignity and independence. His proper work may be bullfighting or fishing or writing, but whatever it is, he does it with consummate skill—he is an artist in the rigging. A man does not gain happiness from his work—not in Melville or Conrad or Hemingway. He does not even find "fulfillment," as Thomas Carlyle would have it. He does not discover there the answers to the mysteries of life. That is not what finding your own reality means. The terrible whiteness, the heart of darkness, the nada—these remain the context of life for all three authors. What is gained from work is the personal revelation of self-integrity (which is not self-righteousness but the feeling of wholeness), and from that derives an awareness of identity and a sense of independence. It is an experience of no little consequence to look deep within yourself and to find there a soul.

The proper work for the narrator of *Omoo* is that of "sailorman," and the novel is constructed on his movement toward that

---

as close to Melville's as that of any other writer. One of the best ways to understand the deeper implications of *Omoo* is to study "Heart of Darkness."

19. "Proper" in this sense means *natural*, the work for which a man seems intended. When he is performing any other work, he appears out of place.

work. Alternately he seeks work and rejects it (or does not find it) until he finds a new ship and goes back to sea. Briefly this pattern can be outlined as follows: the narrator leaves Nukuheva after the inactivity of *Typee* in order to become a sailor again; when the trouble develops on board the *Julia,* he advises the crew against violence and suggests that they all refuse work; he then agrees to help work the ship into Tahiti; a long period of inactivity in the "Calabooza Beretanee" then ensues; he leaves the calabooza and goes to work digging potatoes and tilling the hard soil for the planters Zeke and Shorty; this is obviously the most deadening kind of task for him, and he leaves in Long Ghost's company to loaf and wander over Imeeo; arriving at Partoowye, he seeks employment in the queen's service (Long Ghost's idea), but is rejected; he then encounters the captain of the *Leviathan* and is elated at the prospects of returning to sea. Thus the novel ends as it begins, with the narrator assuming his role as sailor after an interlude in which he has been mostly in an alien surrounding.[20]

Melville's concept of work controlled most of the characterizations in *Omoo*. Long Ghost, for example, can be given no designation in terms of work. He is not really a physician, though he claims to be. Neither is he a sailor. He talks cleverly of many things but he *is* nothing.[21] Like a chameleon he shrewdly assumes the

20. This time, however, he sets out under much more promising circumstances, for the new captain seems himself to be a "sailor-man," whereas Captain Guy certainly was not.

21. Long Ghost was based upon a man named John Troy, whom Melville met aboard the *Lucy Ann.* Troy was not a doctor but merely a steward who had charge of the medical supplies. He did not resign his position after a quarrel with the captain, as it happens in the novel, but was demoted for theft and desertion. Whether Melville knew Troy's background is not entirely clear, but he did portray Long Ghost as a fraud, albeit a jolly and entertaining one. In fact, Long Ghost is the twin brother of another colossal fraud in literature, the hero of Tobias Smollett's novel *The Adventures of Ferdinand Count Fathom*, a book which Po-Po brought the narrator and Long Ghost to read along with *Amelia* and *Peregrine Pickle*. For Smollett's influence on Melville's characterization of Long Ghost, see William B. Dillingham, "Melville's Long Ghost and Smollett's Count Fathom," *American Literature*, XLII (1970), 232–35. Melville also mentioned Count Fathom in

color of his surroundings. His fate may well be that of Lem Hardy.
In fact, Melville strongly hints at the direction in which Long
Ghost is headed when the narrator and Long Ghost set out
from Zeke and Shorty's plantation for Taloo. As is so often the
case, Melville uses clothing to suggest a fundamental aspect of
character:

> We at once put ourselves in traveling trim. Just previous to leaving
> Tahiti, having found my wardrobe reduced to two suits (frock and
> trowsers, both much the worse for wear), I had quilted them to-
> gether for mutual preservation (after a fashion peculiar to sailors);
> engrafting a red frock upon a blue one, and producing thereby
> a choice variety in the way of clothing. This was the extent of my
> wardrobe. Nor was the doctor by any means better off. His im-
> providence had at last driven him to don the nautical garb; but by
> this time, his frock—a light cotton one—had almost given out, and
> he had nothing to replace it. Shorty very generously offered him
> one which was a little less ragged; but the alms was proudly re-
> fused; Long Ghost preferring to assume the ancient costume of
> Tahiti—the *"Roora."* (p. 235)

At this point in the book (before they reach Tamai), the narrator has worn only one kind of clothing—that of the sailor. He has
sewed his suits together and preserved them as best he could. Long
Ghost, on the other hand, has worn at least three kinds of clothing
—that of the physician, that of the sailor, and now that of the
Tahitian native.[22] Significantly Long Ghost tells the narrator at
the end that "he had made up his mind to tarry awhile in Imeeo"
(p. 315). The doctor, who hates *any* kind of work, has been
marked no less than the sailor with the Fa-Fa or Lem Hardy with
his tattoo. The refusal of the captain of the *Leviathan* to take Long
Ghost aboard his ship is a striking parallel to the fate of the dis-

---

White-Jacket, where he says of Mad Jack's drinking: "The vice was in-
veterate; surely, like Ferdinand, Count Fathom, he must have been suckled
at a puncheon" (p. 34).

22. Long Ghost dons the sailor's garb again at Partoowye, a gift of Po-Po's
wife, Arfretee. But this simply indicates the ease with which he shifts roles
in life. None of them are permanent or meaningful to him.

eased sailor. While the narrator has been moving toward his proper work, Long Ghost has been gradually infected by Tahiti.

Consistently in *Omoo* a man's character is revealed by how well (or how poorly) he performs his job. Since the narrator is a "sailor-man," he uses the standards of that particular work to measure other characters by. When he calls one man a real sailor and another a "landsman," he is often describing more than mere walks of life; he is using these contrasting terms in much the same way that Conrad uses "the craft" (or "one of us") as opposed to the outsider or the way in which Hemingway distinguishes between two kinds of doctors in *A Farewell to Arms* or two kinds of bullfighters in *The Sun Also Rises* or two kinds of fishermen in *The Old Man and the Sea*. It is not that one should not be a landsman (although per se the term is often pejorative) so much as it is wrong for a landsman to pretend to be a sailor. In this respect *Omoo* makes essentially the same point as *White-Jacket* about disguises. The narrator describes Captain Guy of the *Julia* as "pale and slender, more like a sickly counting-house clerk than a bluff sea-captain" (p. 6). In almost every comment about Guy, the narrator indicates directly or indirectly (and almost always contemptuously) how unsuited the captain is for the work he is trying to do. He managed to procure command of the *Julia* through "some favoritism or other," rather than through his skill. He was "essentially a lands-man, and though a man of education, no more meant for the sea than a hair-dresser" (p. 10). Melville's scorn for this type was later directed against the captains of the *Virgin* and *Rose Bud* in *Moby-Dick*. For such men as Captain Guy independence and strength of character are impossible. He keeps away from his crew because he realizes they do not respect him. The man who wears Guy's cast-off coat (again the clothing metaphor is significant), Rope-Yarn, is less contemptible than Guy but much like him in his inability to perform well any part of the work of seaman. "Of all landlubbers," he is "the most lubberly and the most miserable" (p. 53). He should be in a baker's shop or in a tavern sipping his ale. Aboard the *Julia* he is ostracized and mistreated by the crew who is entirely unsympathetic with his ineptness and weakness. Ironically he dies ashore in a hospital for sailors. The acting English consul at Papeetee, Wilson, is still another example of a man pretending to be something he is not. The impression which the narrator leaves of Wilson is of a man failing abysmally to do his work. He, as a consul, is as much an impersonator as Guy is as captain and Rope-Yarn as sailor. The mutineers' defiance of his authority frustrates him endlessly. So he keeps on drinking and pretending to be a man.

When a man performs his job effectively, with skill and diligence, the narrator is willing to overlook almost any failing. John Jermin, first mate of the *Julia* and a forerunner of Mad Jack in *White-Jacket*, schemes to take over the ship, drinks excessively, and fights far too much to even resemble an exemplar of virtue. Despite all this and even though Jermin is against the mutineers on the *Julia*, he nevertheless commands the narrator's respect and admiration: "So far as courage, seamanship, and a natural aptitude for keeping riotous spirits in subjection were concerned, no man was better qualified for his vocation than John Jermin" (p. 11). Just how well he performs his work can be seen clearly in at least two episodes. When the savage Mowree, Bembo, tries to run the *Julia* upon a coral reef, the crew attempts to murder him, but Jermin prevents it out of an ingrained sense of responsibility to his job, not out of love for Bembo. A few pages later he reflects his skill as a seaman and his independence when he pilots the *Julia* through an extremely dangerous reef near Tahiti. When the regular pilot fails to appear, Jermin "determined to stand boldly in upon his own responsibility; trusting solely to what he remembered of the harbor on a visit there many years previous. This resolution was characteristic" (p. 98).

A man "qualified for his vocation" cannot, in Melville's thinking, be weak or petty. Jermin is depicted as having "a heart as big as a bullock's; that you saw at a glance" (p. 11). He is without maliciousness even when fighting with his crew or flogging them. Guy and Wilson use him for their own purposes, but it is always clear that he is as unlike them as the narrator is unlike Long Ghost. He is last seen about half-way through the novel as he stands on the bowsprit of the *Julia* and gives the orders that will take his new crew to sea. His final act before leaving is to see to it that the mutineers' sea chests are sent ashore to them "and every thing left therein" (p. 151).

Omoo distinguishes two kinds of people with the self-confidence of John Calvin. Melville's elect are the artists in the rigging. An important question is whether they belong to this select group *because* they find their work and perform it well or whether they find their work only because they are of the elect, men with hearts and souls—the incorruptible. The weight of evidence seems to support the latter alternative. The shadows that pass as men—the Long Ghosts of the world—never find their proper work, not because they do not look but because they *are* ghosts and consequently for them it does not exist. The metaphor of work in *Omoo* is a skillful way of projecting innate character rather than a means of developing a Carlylean philosophy of human potential. *Omoo* is comic rather than tragic not only because the hero retains his own values in the midst of corrupting indolence but because there is little real doubt that he will do otherwise.

APOTHEOSIS

Part III

MARDI: The Sun Also Rises

Chapter 6

The world of *Mardi* is a confusing roundhouse of mirrors, in which the narrator seeks substance and meaning but finds only empty reflections. He enters into this mad world of mirrors with Yillah, a fair maiden whom he takes from Aleema, a pagan priest. For a short time he possesses her in perfect bliss. When she disappears, he is left to search for her, but in vain. Most of the book, then, deals with the narrator's futile efforts to regain Yillah as he searches among the islands of the archipelago of Mardi with his friends: Media, king of Odo; Babbalanja, a philosopher; Yoomy, a poet; and Mohi, a historian. Before he first discovers Yillah, his wanderings have no definite object. After he loses her, he no longer drifts; he then searches specifically if futilely. In *Mardi*, therefore, the hero's life is presented in two stages: he is a wanderer and then a searcher.

What characterizes the narrator through about the first forty chapters is his lack of a definite purpose in life. He is merely restless and isolated from others. Aboard the *Arcturion* he states, "there was no soul a magnet to mine; none with whom to mingle sympathies" (p. 4). He complains that there are none with whom he can "talk sentiment or philosophy" (p. 5). Though he works as hard as the next man, he is never accepted by the crew. Only old Jarl, a taciturn Skyeman, wants to befriend him. And even Jarl seems to be attracted to him chiefly because he is different; he thinks Jarl had "taken me for ... Charles Edward the Pretender, who, like the Wandering Jew, may yet be a vagrant" (p. 14). Such an endless wanderer he is indeed, not unlike the Wandering Jew or even the youthful heroes of Melville's other early books.

When he finds Yillah, she becomes the incarnation of a dream—an indefinite vision or longing transformed into flesh. He realizes at last *why* he has been so restless, why he has wandered "over the wide watery world ... from isle to isle, from sea to sea" (p. 143). He sees her as "the earthly semblance of that sweet vision, that haunted my earliest thoughts" (p. 158). Her role is that of the strange and beautiful "faery's child" in Keats's "La Belle Dame sans Merci." The knight of Keats's poem discovers a beautiful woman in his travels, falls desperately in love with her, and goes with her to a secluded retreat. There he makes love to her, falls asleep, and dreams of all those who in the past have suffered from losing the beautiful lady. When the knight awakes, he finds her gone and his life as empty and desolate as the wintry hillside on which he sits alone. The meaning of Melville's Yillah is no more definite than Keats's La Belle Dame, though some critics have tried to sum up her allegorical meaning very precisely. Newton Arvin, Richard Chase, and Leslie Fiedler all associate Yillah with Melville's idealistic view of woman, or more specifically, with Elizabeth Shaw before Melville married her. After marriage she could no longer seem so beautiful or desirable; so, in effect, she "disappeared" as Yillah does in the novel.[1] Others, like James E. Miller, Jr., see Yillah as innocence, which when lost can never be

1. Newton Arvin, *Herman Melville* (New York, 1950), pp. 95–96; Richard Chase, *Herman Melville: A Critical Study* (New York, 1949), pp. 33–34; Leslie A. Fiedler, *Love and Death in the American Novel* (New

recovered.[2] It seems to me unnecessary, or perhaps even unwise, to think of Yillah in any but the most general terms. Of primary importance is what she means to the narrator, not to the reader, and to him she is the concrete realization of whatever it is he has been seeking. At last he thinks he has filled the emptiness in his life. His wanderings over, he finds an islet close to Odo and there "decided to dwell" (p. 188). But paradise on earth is by necessity short-lived. As early as *Typee* that theme is reflected in Tommo's realization that he must push off from the lee shore he has found.

For a time, then, the narrator's state of mind is that of Keats's knight when he found the beautiful faery's child: "Sped the hours, the days, the one brief moment of our joys. Fairy bower in the fair lagoon, scene of sylvan ease and heart's repose" (p. 193). Like the knight, he dreams one night a terrible dream and awakes to find Yillah gone. From that moment he becomes the searcher. Whereas the wanderer of Melville's fiction feels often a "damp, drizzly November" in his soul and then compulsively escapes to a new setting, the searcher is a man preoccupied with a single, well-defined aim. In the case of Ahab it is to seek out and destroy the white whale; with Taji it is to recover the lost Yillah. The wanderer is the true seeker because his mind is not closed; he seeks answers to questions that profoundly disturb him. The searcher believes he knows the answers. His mind is closed tight with a monomania that sends him madly in pursuit of a tangible object. The wanderer recognizes that ambiguity, not final answers, lies at the heart of life. To put it another way, the wanderer can recognize a symbol as such; for the searcher the symbol merges with the thing it symbolizes, and in his monomania he can no longer distinguish the thing from the abstract qualities it suggests. After years of wandering Taji finds a concrete image, a symbol, for all that he has been desiring. The magic incarnation takes place, and thereafter his vision is distorted.

York, 1960), p. 297. See also Mildred K. Travis, "*Mardi*: Melville's Allegory of Love," *Emerson Society Quarterly*, No. 43 (1966), pp. 86–87.

2. *A Reader's Guide to Herman Melville* (New York, 1962), pp. 36–53.

Yillah then is not merely a girl; she *is* his paradise on earth, and to recover her is to find perfection, tranquility, and fulfillment.

For the first time in Melville's fiction, therefore, this important distinction is suggested between two vital stages in the life of the hero. The two phases are delineated more powerfully and more convincingly in *Moby-Dick* through two separate characters, Ishmael and Ahab. Inferior though *Mardi* certainly is, however, it gives a glimpse of the terrible metamorphosis within a single character. Ahab has already become a titanic madman when the novel opens, but in *Mardi* we witness the birth of such a character. The series of references to the narrator's "deaths" prepare the way for his new role. When he and Jarl desert the *Arcturion*, they carefully work out a plan so that the captain and crew will think them dead. Then they are taken for ghosts when they board the *Parki* and discover Samoa and his shrewish wife Annatoo. Again in Chapter 38 they appear as ghosts, this time to each other as they observe the sea alive with "pallid white color" (p. 121).

As long as he plays the part of wanderer, the narrator has no name, but with his birth to a new role he takes a name worthy of the larger than human task he later assumes. After arriving at Odo (and almost concurrent with his losing Yillah) the narrator comes to be known as Taji, a demigod in Mardian lore whose dwelling place was the sun. After Yillah is torn from him, his agony and ravings prefigure Ahab's when homeward bound from his first encounter with Moby Dick and suffering the loss of his leg, "his torn body and gashed soul bled into one another."[3] When Ahab lost his leg to the whale's "direful wrath," the sun shone "as if at a birth or a bridal."[4] A birth indeed it was—the birth of the searcher. In his hammock he was "a raving lunatic"; later when he came from his cabin outwardly calm he was a changed man who "in his hidden self, raved on."[5] Similarly Taji the searcher is born when

3. *Moby-Dick*, ed. Harrison Hayford and Hershel Parker (New York, 1967), p. 160.

4. Ibid., p. 159.

5. Ibid., pp. 160, 161.

Yillah is torn from his bridal bower. Like Ahab he suffers almost unendurable agony: "For a time I raved. Then, falling into outer repose, lived for a space in moods and reveries, with eyes that knew no closing . . ." (p. 194). Even the outer repose is broken when in those evenings he dreams of what he has lost: "Then came over me the wild dream Yillah; and, for a space, like a madman, I raved. It seemed as if the mysterious damsel must still be there; the rescue yet to be achieved" (p. 306). As the pursuit of Moby Dick preoccupies Ahab, so the recovery of Yillah with Taji.

Melville was clearly working his way toward his most convincing and stirring portrayal of the searching hero, Ahab. Both characters seek to accomplish the same fundamental goal—the destruction of evil. By finding and killing the white whale, Ahab believes he can somehow destroy the force of evil which has long plagued him in many forms. Taji believes that by regaining the white maiden all imperfection in his life will disappear and he can live in a paradise free from evil. Their aims are humanly impossible, but they elevate themselves while pursuing their suicidal course, knowing that it is suicidal but convinced that the hand of destiny will not let them waver. "Fain would I hurl off this Dionysius that rides me," says Taji. "My thoughts crush me down till I groan; in far fields I hear the song of the reaper, while I slave and faint in this cell. The fever runs through me like lava; my hot brain burns like a coal; and like many a monarch, I am less to be envied, than the veriest hind in the land" (p. 368). Like Ahab, Taji is compared to Prometheus: "In all the universe is but one original; and the very suns must to their source for their fire; and we Prometheuses must to them for ours; which, when had, only perpetual Vestal tending will keep alive" (p. 229). Later he cries: "My own mad brood of eagles devours me" (p. 368). Once having a glimpse of "the golden haven," however, he must search on even though it never be gained. "Yet, in bold quest thereof, better to sink in boundless deeps, than float on vulgar shoals; and give me, ye gods, an utter wreck, if wreck I do" (p. 557).

Although he never floats in vulgar shoals, it is not clearly estab-

lished that Taji ever sinks in boundless deeps either. In fact, critics
have never agreed on just what happens to Taji at the end of
Mardi. His state of mind at that point approaches madness; he
recklessly ignores the limits that bind ordinary mortals. "I am the
hunter, that never rests!" he cries. "The hunter without a home!
She I seek, still flies before; and I will follow, though she lead me
beyond the reef; through sunless seas; and into night and death.
Her, will I seek, through all the isles and stars; and find her,
whate'er betide! . . . Then, then! my heart grew hard, like flint;
and black, like night; and sounded hollow to the hand I clenched.
Hyenas filled me with their laughs; death-damps chilled my brow;
I prayed not, but blasphemed" (pp. 638–39). When he fails to find
Yillah on Hautia's island, he heads desperately for the open sea. To
Mohi's plea that he return with them to Serenia, he says: "By Oro,
I will steer my own fate, old man" (p. 654). Yoomy admonishes
him not to commit "the last, last crime," but he steers the small
boat for "that outer ocean." Mohi and Yoomy jump from the boat
and swim for land. Taji's final words are "Now, I am my own
soul's emperor; and my first act is abdication! Hail! realm of
shades!" Then "turning my prow into the racing tide, which
seized me like a hand omnipotent, I darted through," with the
three avenging sons of old Aleema in hot pursuit (p. 654).

If Taji's actions at the book's end are not suicidal, it is difficult to
say what they are. Tyrus Hillway and others have agreed that
Taji's "abdication" and the "last, last crime" Yoomy speaks of both
refer clearly to suicide.[6] Indeed, the urge to self-destruction is a
strong element in the character of all three of Melville's searching
heroes, Taji, Ahab, and Pierre. But *Mardi* is the only one of the
three novels told by the searcher himself. The reader is confronted
with the illogicality of a dead man narrating his own story. Consequently there is a strong temptation to interpret the ending in
such a way as to keep Taji alive—a temptation that may result in
distortion. Another way of approaching the problem is to assume,

6. Tyrus Hillway, "Taji's Abdication in Herman Melville's *Mardi*,"
American Literature, XVI (1944), 204–207.

as does Milton R. Stern, that the book lacks a definite plan, and that Melville simply blundered with his point of view.[7]

To be sure, *Mardi* is a book with many flaws and the narrative point of view is unquestionably one of them. However, the mistake Melville made with his point of view was not, it seems to me, in failing to realize soon enough that he was going to kill his hero and then finding it too late to go back and change his method of narration. Instead it was a failure to execute successfully an extremely ambitious and original concept of narration. Scattered references throughout the first part of the book suggest that Taji did live through his ordeal and is now retelling his story. In the first chapter, for example, he says: "Never before had the ocean appeared so monotonous; thank fate, never since" (p. 4). In the same chapter he looks back over his escape from the *Arcturion* and states that "were I placed in the same situation again, I would repeat the thing I did then" (p. 7). When he tells in Chapter 7 how the *Arcturion* had sunk some time after he and Jarl deserted it, he is obviously relating information he could have obtained only after *returning* from Mardi. The problem, then, is to account for a first-person narrator who is definitely *retelling* the story of a series of adventures that ended in his death.

An immediate solution might be to consider the point of view an example of an illogical but entirely acceptable device frequently used in poetry—the "voice from the grave" technique. Emily Dickinson liked to describe how she felt when she died or what it was like to be in the grave. Hardy had corpses talking pessimistically of channel firing that disturbed their rest. Housman had his speaker ask from the grave if his team was still plowing. Although seldom used in fiction, there seems no reason why the device should offend logic more in a work as highly imaginative and unrealistic as *Mardi* than it would in poetry. The relative degree of effectiveness, of course, would be another question.

What Melville was attempting was much more complex. At the

7. *The Fine Hammered Steel of Herman Melville* (Urbana, 1957), pp. 69–70.

novel's end he wanted Taji to be *both* dead and alive. Taji's progression from wanderer to searcher necessitates a series of "deaths," which represent stages in his transformation. The "last, last crime" may well be actual suicide, but it is also the act of Ahab refusing to help Captain Gardiner of the *Rachel* to search for his lost son. It is, in other words, the final act of renunciation of life and humanity. As the searching hero proceeds on his unswerving course, he moves further and further from normal humanity until as a human being he "dies." If this process results in monomania and cruelty, it is also the means of achieving Promethean stature. Such is the meaning of Ishmael's paradoxical statement about Bulkington: "Bear thee grimly, demigod! Up from the spray of thy ocean-perishing—straight up, leaps thy apotheosis!"[8] Taji, at the end of *Mardi*, has *become* that demigod whose name he so casually took, and he does, indeed, "perish." He abdicates, gives up his life among humanity, but from that "ocean perishing" comes the rebelling, blaspheming, greater-than-human hero who, like Prometheus, must suffer eternally, but whose suffering lifts him above the level of ordinary mankind.

The narrator of *Mardi*, therefore, is no ordinary mortal, nor does his voice come merely from the grave. It reverberates from constellation to constellation throughout the universe. Taji must play out his part forever, for he lost the comfortable advantage of death when his humanity died within him. *Mardi* had to be "an allegorical romance," a strange, unrealistic book to accommodate such a hero. This strangeness results largely from the fact that Taji has to play two parts at once—the narrator who must reconstruct events that took place in the past and which changed him drastically and the speaker who must suggest his new role at the very moment he tells of the past. It is because of this situation that Taji describes Mardi both as an actual archipelago and—almost in the same breath—as a group of planets in space. The search for Yillah takes place concurrently on the islands of Mardi and throughout

8. *Moby-Dick*, p. 98.

the boundless spaces of the universe. The ship Taji deserts is called the *Arcturion*, after the star. Samoa takes Jarl and Taji to be "a couple of men from the moon" (p. 86). Taji frequently looks at the stars, and in Chapter 58 he cries: "Oh stars! oh eyes, that see me, wheresoe'er I roam . . . tell me Sybils, what I am.—Wondrous worlds on worlds! Lo, round and round me, shining, awful spells: all glorious, vivid constellations . . ." (p. 179). In the chapter on "Dreams" Taji imagines himself a frigate traveling through the "boundless expanses" of space (p. 367). The scores of references throughout *Mardi* to stars, constellations, and planets reflect, as Merrell R. Davis has shown, a widespread interest in astronomy at the time Melville was writing.[9] But they also expand Taji's role from that of a mere human being searching on earth to a kind of avatar traveling through seas of space.

Taji is, as the title of Chapter 54 indicates, "A Gentleman from the Sun," and "as the sun, by influence divine, wheels through the Ecliptic; threading Cancer, Leo, Pisces, and Aquarius; so, by some mystic impulse am I moved, to this fleet progress, through the groups in white-reefed Mardi's zone" (p. 556).[10] This comparison of the archipelago of Mardi with the Zodiac and of Taji with the sun that travels through the twelve signs is maintained throughout most of the book. Together Taji and his friends visit twelve island kingdoms (the group breaks up before Taji goes on to Flozella) :[11] Valapee, Juam, Ohonoo, Mondoldo, Maramma, Pimminee, Diranda, Dominora, Vivenza, Hooloomooloo, Bonovona, and Serenia.

In most of these realms the ruler or the populace reflects qualities (often negative rather than positive) traditionally associated in

9. *Melville's "Mardi": A Chartless Voyage* (New Haven, 1952), p. 67.

10. Davis describes Taji's journey as "an imaginary tour through a Milky Way of South Sea islands" (p. 69).

11. However, they do visit other places which are not described: "Over that tideless sea we sailed; and landed right, and landed left; but the maiden never found" (p. 554). In addition, they visit a few small islands, such as Doxodox's island, with no inhabitants or only one.

astrology with the sign that place represents. For example, the first visit, to Valapee, corresponds to the sun's visitation to the constellation of Aries, the Ram. This island, which is also called the Isle of Yams, is ruled by an impulsive youth named Peepi, "one of the most unreliable of beings" (p. 203). In several ways he reflects the unfavorable side of the Aries type, who, according to Louis MacNeice, "tends to be an impetuous juvenile."[12] Next Taji and the others visit the island of Juam, which would be in the order of astrological signs, that of Taurus, the Bull. MacNeice comments that "to the layman it may seem comic that Taurus should be feminine. . . . The hostile Robert Eisler even suggests that he was never a bull, only an ox, and quotes the ancient Roman champion of astrology Termicus Maternus to the effect that this sign is responsible for the birth of impotent people and perverts."[13] This description hits close to the mark, for the young monarch of Juam, Donjalolo, possesses a comeliness "so feminine, that he was sometimes called 'Fonoo,' or the Girl" (p. 216). He has thirty wives, one for each night of the month, but he has no child—"Not more effeminate Sardanapalus, than he" (p. 223). From Juam the travelers go on to Ohonoo, which is actually a kind of double island, "midway cloven down to the sea" (p. 272), and thus suggestive of the third sign of the zodiac, Gemini, the twins. Appropriately the "tutelar deity" of Ohonoo is Keevi, the god of thieves. The ruling planet of Gemini is Mercury, which is often associated with thieves in astrology.

Such connections of islands and rulers with astrological types can be seen in varying degrees throughout most of the twelve visits. Knowing that the moon rules the sign of Cancer, an astrologist would not be at all surprised to find that King Borabolla of Mondoldo—where Taji and his friends pay their fourth visit—is a fine example of the "moon child" with his jolliness and great round

12. *Astrology* (London, 1964), p. 81. Jerryl L. Keane, in *Practical Astrology* (West Nyack, N. Y., 1967), says the negative Arian "persists in a muddle of activity without purpose or direction" (p. 27).

13. MacNeice, p. 83.

face. The powerful Pontiff of Maramma, Hivohitee, who demands "large tribute . . . from the neighboring shores," is strongly suggestive of the type of Leo, the fifth sign of the Zodiac. In fact, Taji says that Hivohitee "lays claim to King Leo's share of the spoils, and secures it" (p. 353). On Diranda, which represents the sign of Libra, the Balances, the visitors find a perfect balance worked out by King Hello and Piko so that the population will not grow too rapidly nor be diminished too suddenly through wars. These remarkable kings have discovered that they can keep the population in perfect equilibrium by killing off just the right number through frequent tournaments of combat. On Dominora, the eighth place of Taji's visit and thus the sign of Scorpio (ruled by Mars), Taji and his group meet King Bello. He is the very type of Mars, "a testy, quarrelsome, rapacious old monarch; the indefatigable breeder of contentions and wars" (p. 466). Although most of the characteristics found in the various rulers or people of these islands reflect undesirable traits associated with the sign they live under, the people of Serenia, the twelfth place, suggest for the first time positive qualities. The fish of pisces, the twelfth sign, were also an early symbol of Christianity and MacNeice writes that "the Piscean tends to 'lose himself' in love."[14] The gentle, melancholy people of Serenia represent well the Piscean type.

Melville's working out of a journey through Mardi in terms of the sun's progress through the zodiac is much more than an elaborate metaphor. It is an attempt to break down the barrier of time and show the past—the actual journey Taji made through the islands—and the present—Taji's endless journey through space—in the same moment. Taji becomes a Sisyphus occupied through all eternity in his painful repetition that never leads to fulfillment. Or he is an Ixion going round and round in an endless course.

My reading of Taji as a searcher in space is close to the interpretation of H. Bruce Franklin, who sees him in "the role of an astronomical avatar," more particularly, a Whistonian comet traveling

14. Ibid., p. 105.

eternally through the universe.[15] My view differs sharply from Franklin's, however, on the issue of Taji's guilt. "The narrator is in fact a Whistonian damned soul," writes Franklin. "His damnation consists of repeating over and over again an act of moral abdication and being regarded, after each abdication, as a supernatural being."[16] I cannot agree that Taji is doomed to his particular form of eternal repetition—searching for Yillah—because of some specific act of sin. He killed the priest Aleema, and some critics consequently feel that he is the cause of the deaths of Jarl and Samoa since Almeea's sons were avenging their father's death on Taji's friends.[17] But *Mardi* is not a book about morality. It sets no standards and punishes no one for being a sinner. In contrast to critics who see Melville establishing some kind of norm of moral behavior by which to measure his characters, Charles Feidelson, Jr., deserves to be heard:

> Taji's decision to continue the quest may be a "crime," as one of his companions alleges, but if so it is an unavoidable crime, woven into the texture of human existence. Here again, the fact that his quest is inaugurated by an act of violence is no index of Melville's ultimate judgment on him. The death of the priest Aleema is not a clear case of unjustifiable homicide. On the contrary, Taji's sense of guilt is part of his growing sense of the ambiguity of human motives in general and of his own in particular. His self-doubt is the counterpart of the inherent ambiguity of his object, Yillah, for whom he committed the deed. Thus the three vengeful pursuers, who dog him throughout his journey and follow him out to sea at the end, are inseparable from his own pursuit. Their presence does not brand him as a criminal but is the seal of his humanity.[18]

The role of blasphemous, monomaniacal undying titan in which Taji is finally cast is not a part he is forced to play as punishment

15. *The Wake of the Gods: Melville's Mythology* (Stanford, 1963), p. 40.

16. Ibid., p. 41.

17. See, for example, Stern, p. 104. According to John Seelye, "By that act . . . he [Taji] seems to damn himself to failure from the very first" (*Melville: The Ironic Diagram*, Evanston, 1970, p. 35).

18. *Symbolism and American Literature* (Chicago, 1953), p. 172.

for his sins so much as it is punishment for exercising with the strongest possible vigor man's greatest virtues—love of perfection and strength of will. In this black testament of pessimism, the more the hero pursues his highest human urges, the less human he becomes.[19]

The problems in point of view are by no means solved, however, even after it is established that Melville keeps his narrator alive (if metamorphosed). For the journey from wanderer to searcher (and to searching avatar) is a one-way trip. If in the final action of the book Taji is not in the process of committing actual suicide, he has in fact removed himself so far from humanity that it is hardly possible to think of him as becoming calm enough to go back and narrate his story. Perhaps the most serious flaw in the method of narration, however, is that Taji all but drops out of sight during the journey to various islands of Mardi. He seldom speaks to his group of fellow travelers. Only occasionally do they recognize his presence among them; and when he has to speak of himself, he often avoids the first-person pronoun in favor of "Taji." Consequently, his driving compulsion is not kept constantly before the reader, and the search for Yillah that supposedly motivates the entire group frequently resembles a leisurely pleasure tour more than a monomaniac's wild striving to find what he has lost. This difficulty results from at least two major sources. One was Melville's increasing interest in another character, Babbalanja, who comes to overshadow the narrator. The ending with all of its sound and fury signifies a great deal less than it should because Taji has long since become secondary to Babbalanja. In addition, Taji's presence seems to fade because Melville found it necessary to create

19. William Ellery Sedgwick, in _Herman Melville: The Tragedy of Mind_ (Cambridge, Mass., 1944), makes this point succinctly: "The great man, the fairest possible semblance of humanity, is impelled to achieve a noble and impossible ideal, and in the very effort to achieve this ideal destroys the fairest semblance of humanity" (p. 58). John Bernstein, in _Pacifism and Rebellion in the Writings of Herman Melville_ (The Hague, 1964), states that "the more intensely Taji pursues Yillah, the more he becomes immersed in the evil which he seeks to avoid" (p. 55).

greater aesthetic distance in the later parts of the novel. Taji's changing role entails progressive isolation, both from the group with whom he is journeying and from the reader. Consequently, although it is supposedly still his voice we hear relating what others say and do, as a character he fades into the distance and becomes shadowy. Melville was successful in creating distance between reader and narrator and thus in dehumanizing and isolating Taji. The cost of this success, however, was far too great; the effect was achieved at the expense of forceful and convincing characterization.

Babbalanja and Taji are closely related. Babbalanja is Taji's former self—step by step he follows behind, becoming what Taji has been. The wanderer is never really absent from *Mardi*; for at that precise time when Taji loses Yillah and thus changes roles from wanderer to searcher, Babbalanja is introduced. He is the new wanderer, filling the place vacated by Taji. His state of mind at this point is reminiscent of the early Taji. He wants to accompany Taji on his pursuit of Yillah, but she is not *his* Yillah. In fact he is merely a follower, seeking some truth or intangible goal without knowing what it is. Taji says, "He murmured deep concern for my loss, the sincerest sympathy; and pressing my hand more than once, said lowly, 'Your pursuit is mine, noble Taji. Where'er you search, I follow'" (p. 197). He is an Ishmael who has decided to accompany an Ahab, even though his attitude toward the white object pursued is far different from his leader's. Babbalanja seeks not a white whale or a white maiden, but "the mystery that lieth beyond; the elements of the tear which much laughter provoketh; that which is beneath the seeming; the precious pearl within the shaggy oyster. I probe the circle's center; I seek to evolve the inscrutable" (p. 352).

The "precious pearl within the shaggy oyster" that Babbalanja seeks turns out to be religious certitude. When he discovers and accepts the religion of Serenia, he believes he has found his pearl. In using the pearl to suggest heaven or religious fulfillment, Melville was echoing Jesus's words to the multitude in St. Matthew: "Again, the kingdom of heaven is like unto a merchantman, seeking goodly pearls: Who, when he had found one pearl of great price, went and sold all that he had, and bought it" (13:45–47). Babbalanja's religious conversion is of crucial importance in _Mardi_. Since he is as important a character as the narrator, his happy conversion may appear to some to offset the pessimism suggested by Taji's futile search.[20] Or one may consider Serenia a deceptive illusion, and thus Babbalanja's "conversion" as unmeaningful. Richard Chase, for example, has written that Melville wanted to show Serenia as unacceptable: "It was too mild, too wistful, too innocent. . . . And Serenia's god might turn out (as he does in _The Confidence Man_) to be a dull little man in a white suit who looks wise but is afraid of dirt."[21] Or one may view Babbalanja's conversion as inconsistent and feeble, as does Stern, who writes that by the end of the book Babbalanja has become a "crashing bore" and his retirement to Serenia is "the anti-climactic picture of the philosopher who dwells by the side of the road . . . and is a friend to Man."[22]

These divergent views suggest frequent ways in which Babbalanja's acceptance of Alma (Christ) is interpreted—as an inspiring and optimistic aspect of the book, as an indication of the superficiality and narrowness of religion, or as merely another weakness in a book already marked by flaws. What seems lacking in these as well as in many other interpretations is the recognition that Babbalanja and Taji are closely connected characters.[23] What happens to Babbalanja has already happened to Taji; the present for one is the future for the other. Babbalanja's conversion, therefore, cannot be viewed as a separate and unique case but must be seen in the light of Taji's discovery of Yillah.

20. See for example Seelye, who feels that Babbalanja's conversion "is posed as an alternative to the life-in-death satanism chosen by Taji . . ." (p. 39). See also Lewis Mumford, _Herman Melville: A Study of His Life and Vision_, rev. ed. (New York, 1962), pp. 55–70.

21. _Herman Melville_, p. 20.

22. _The Fine Hammered Steel of Herman Melville_, p. 140.

23. Davis, for example, remarks that "The conversion of Babbalanja is one story; the endless quest of the Narrator is another" (p. 184).

The connection between Serenia and Yillah is strongly implied through the pearl imagery. Babbalanja seeks "the precious pearl within the shaggy oyster," and thinks he finds it in Serenia. Taji seeks Yillah, who is frequently associated with a pearl. She wears a "rose-coloured pearl on her bosom," which seems to glow when Taji is near her and which haunts him after he has lost her; and when Hautia invites him to dive for pearls, he knows she is referring to Yillah: "but did'st ever dive in deep waters, Taji? Did'st ever see where pearls grow?—To the cave!" (p. 650). There Hautia challenges him to dive for all he desires, including the "last lost hope of man." "Dive thou," she says, "and bring up one pearl if thou canst" (p. 651). His "one pearl," Yillah, is forever lost to him, however. He plunges "down, down! down, down, in the clear, sparkling water," but "uprose empty handed" (p. 651). Since Taji finds a precious pearl and irretrievably loses it, it is reasonable to suppose that Babbalanja's great pearl—what he finds in Serenia— will similarly be lost to him.[24] When the novel ends, Babbalanja has just reached that point which Taji reached by Chapter 52 ("Taji Retires from the World"). Babbalanja also retires from the world, and he believes his wanderings over, just as Taji had when he discovered Yillah. The language used to describe Taji's bower of bliss clearly foreshadows Babbalanja's state of paradisiacal contentment on Serenia: "Often I thought that Paradise had overtaken me on earth, and that Yillah was verily an angel, and hence the mysteries that hallowed her" (p. 193).[25] Another hint of the similar function of Yillah to Serenia is offered through the book's flower symbolism. According to Merrell R. Davis, Yillah's name "appears as a possible anagram for 'lily' or 'lily of the valley.' "[26]

24. Sedgwick suggests that Yillah is a symbol of "spiritual joy in harmony with sensuous delight" (p. 50).

25. In Chapter 43 Yillah is described as "like a saint from a shrine" (p. 136).

26. Davis, p. 137. See also Davis's "The Flower Symbolism in *Mardi*," *Modern Language Quarterly*, 11 (1941), 625–38. In Chapter 101 Yoomy refers to Yillah as "the lily you seek" (p. 309).

Like the pearl the lily of the valley has traditional Biblical associations, and thus both seem related to Serenia.

Babbalanja's conversion, then, can hardly be the cause for great rejoicing. At best his contentment on Serenia can only be temporary. Melville leaves him at the point of his greatest happiness but nevertheless plots his future course carefully in the reader's mind. Babbalanja's next step is frighteningly clear. Taji has set the pattern. He will enjoy his unquestioning contentment for a short time, awake one morning to find it disappeared, and spend the rest of his life as a searcher in frantic pursuit. We do not know what tangible form his own Yillah will take, but whatever form, he will never regain it. In every respect Babbalanja belongs among those sensitive, probing heroes of Melville's fiction; it would be all but inconceivable that Melville meant him to attain what is clearly unattainable—the permanent earthly paradise, the "lee shore."

A great deal of psychological preparation takes place in the wanderers of Melville's fiction who arrive at what might be called their moment of certainty. Ahab suffered greatly and was plagued by the world's evil before he found his "answer"—destroy the white whale and evil will be destroyed. Taji says that he was haunted by some vague vision from his earliest years and that Yillah becomes the "earthly semblance" of that vision (p. 158). Babbalanja's moment of certainty comes when he arrives at Serenia. There is really nothing new in the message Babbalanja hears from the old man on Serenia. He has heard it all before even though the manner and humility of the old man seem new. Through the philosopher Bardianna, Babbalanja is close to Alma's teaching throughout the book.[27] Long before his conversion on Serenia he urges a simple belief in God: "Ah! let us Mardians quit this insanity. Let us be content with the theology in the grass and the flower, in seed-time and harvest. Be it enough for us to know that Oro indubitably is"

---

27. Merlin Bowen, in *The Long Encounter* (Chicago, 1960), makes this same point: "Babbalanja finds little here that he has not already known and admired in the teachings of Bardianna, the 'antique pagan.' But coming to him now, in the midst of his despair, it strikes him with new force" (p. 208).

(p. 428). However, he is not psychologically ready to accept his own simple prescription until his doubts have worn him down and his need is overwhelming. But when the need is met and the hero reaches that moment of certainty when doubts disappear and he thinks he is nearest to truth—then he is further from it than ever. It is as Taji himself says in Chapter 97: "Things nearest are furthest off. Though your ear be next-door to your brain, it is forever removed from your sight. Man has a more comprehensive view of the moon, than the man in the moon himself. We know the moon is round; he only infers it" (pp. 296–97). So it must be with Babbalanja and his "conversion."

This is not to say that the values of Serenia are shallow or corrupt any more than is Father Mapple's great sermon in *Moby-Dick*. Melville's description of Serenia is not ironic but genuine. As Ronald Mason has put it, Melville treats Serenia "tenderly," as if he *wished* it could be the final answer to Babbalanja's problems and the world's ills.[28] The Serenias of man's world are not wrong but only sadly inadequate and thus temporary. When Babbalanja awakes and finds his illusion shattered, he will no longer be the same. He will pursue his lost Alma to the world's corners, but the pearl he thought he had within his grasp will never be regained.

In relating Babbalanja's fate to Taji's, Melville was illustrating one of the central ideas of *Mardi*—that which seems separate and unique is merely a part of something else. This concept of oneness is established early in the book when the narrator says: "Thus all generations are blended: and heaven and earth of one kin: the hierarchies of seraphs in the uttermost skies; the thrones and principalities in the zodiac; the shades that roam throughout space; the nations and families, flocks and folds of the earth; one and all, brothers in essence—oh, be we then brothers indeed! All things form but one whole" (p. 12). In his search for oneness Taji time and again expresses his conviction that "many, many souls are in

28. *The Spirit Above the Dust* (London, 1951), p. 61.

me" (p. 367). He feels flowing through his veins the same blood
of countless other human beings of ages past:

> But for me, I was at the subsiding of the Deluge, and helped swab
> the ground, and build the first house. With the Israelites, I fainted
> in the wilderness; was in court, when Solomon outdid all the
> judges before him. I, it was, who suppressed the lost work of
> Manetho, on the Egyptian theology, as containing mysteries not to
> be revealed to posterity, and things at war with the canonical
> scriptures; I, who originated the conspiracy against the purple
> murderer, Domitian; I, who in the senate moved, that great and
> good Aurelian be emperor. I instigated the abdication of Diocle-
> tian, and Charles the Fifth; I touched Isabella's heart that she
> hearkened to Columbus. I am he, that from the king's minions hid
> the Charter in the old oak at Hartford; I harbored Goffe and
> Whalley: I am the leader of the Mohawk masks, who in the Old
> Commonwealth's harbor, overboard threw the East India Com-
> pany's Souchong; I am the Veiled Persian Prophet; I, the man in
> the iron mask; I, Junius. (p. 297)

Similarly Babbalanja frequently voices the same idea, that "in
one life-time we live a hundred lives" (p. 457). Before his conversion on Serenia, he tells King Abrazza: "We are full of ghosts and
spirits; we are as grave-yards full of buried dead, that start to life
before us. And all our dead sires, verily, are in us; *that* is their
immortality. From sire to son, we go on multiplying corpses in
ourselves; for all of which, are resurrections. Every thought's a
soul of some past poet, hero, sage" (pp. 593–94). So it is that Babbalanja and Bardianna are one. When chided that he constantly
quotes Bardianna but seldom contributes any original thoughts,
Babbalanja answers: "I do not so much quote Bardianna, as Bardianna quoted me, though he flourished before me. . . . The catalogue
of true thoughts is but small. . . . They were in us, before we were
born. The truest poets are but mouth-pieces; and some men are
duplicates of each other; I see myself in Bardianna" (p. 397). And
much later in the book he says: "The first man's thoughts were
as ours" (p. 578).

This blending of past into present and one soul into another smacks of Emersonian or Whitmanian Transcendentalism. Nothing could be further from Melville's mind. *Mardi* is Emerson's *Nature* turned inside out. Emerson's favorite idea of a man-centered universe and his repeated insistence upon the unity that underlies diversity led him to unqualified optimism. If Melville seems to be making the same points, his conclusion is diametrically opposite. As Charles Feidelson, Jr., astutely points out, "For Emerson, what could be more 'celestial' " (than the concept expressed in his poem "Uriel" that "Line in nature is not found; / Unit and universe are round") and "For Melville, what could be more infernal?"[29]

Mardi is an infernal book, for the merging of time and souls signifies not unity and purpose but chaos and ambiguity much like the calm which the narrator describes in Chapter 16: "This inert blending and brooding of all things seemed gray chaos in conception" (p. 48). Furthermore, Taji and Babbalanja labor to show how men's thoughts are connected and how one man is a complex of past souls, but they stress equally man's loneliness, his inability to know another. As Babbalanja puts it: "the entire merit of a man can never be made known; nor the sum of his demerits, if he have them. We are only known by our names; as letters sealed up, we but read each other's superscriptions" (p. 394). And later, quoting Bardianna, Babbalanja says of man: "He stands alone. We are every thing to ourselves, but how little to others. What are others to us?" (p. 577). The universal unity expressed in *Mardi*, then, is more insidious than glorious. Men may be brothers, but they can never *feel* like brothers. To be lonely within a family is to suffer the worst loneliness.

Within this framework of interrelatedness, characters and places become echoes and reflections of one another.[30] The beautiful

29. *Symbolism and American Literature*, p. 170.

30. William Braswell, in *Melville's Religious Thought* (Durham, 1943), argues that the five main characters of *Mardi* make up a kind of single com-

green isle of Nora-Bamma (described in Chapter 87), which is inhabited by "dreamers" who "seek oblivion for the past, and ecstasies to come" (p. 265) and whose surrounding waters are calm "like unto Oro's everlasting serenity," is strangely like Serenia. The youth who seeks Oro on Maramma, rejecting a guide and clinging "to that legend of the Peak" only to find death, is a reflection of Taji in his "chartless voyage."[31] Much more basic, however, is the connection between Yillah and Hautia and between the three avenging sons of Aleema and the three heralds of Hautia. Throughout his search Taji thinks of Yillah and Hautia as opposites: "Yillah was all beauty, and innocence; my crown of felicity; my heaven below;—and Hautia, my whole heart abhorred. Yillah I sought; Hautia sought me. One, openly beckoned me here; the other dimly allured me there. Yet now was I wildly dreaming to find them together" (p. 643). On Hautia's island he does, in a sense, find them together, for Yillah has merged with Hautia, and Taji discovers "in some wild way, Hautia had made a captive of Yillah" (p. 649).[32] He has come upon the essential truth that *all* things are ambiguously and sometimes insidiously related. Instead of recognizing that Yillah can no longer exist for him in pure essence, that she is drowned within Hautia, Taji plunges ahead in his futile search. What Taji realizes on Flozella but will not accept—that "in some mysterious way seemed Hautia and Yillah connected" (p. 643)—is prepared for through the periodical reappearances of Aleema's avenging sons and Hautia's heralds. These six shadowy characters function to blur clear-cut distinctions between Yillah and Hautia.

---

posite mind or soul, each symbolizing a different aspect (pp. 87–88). Bowen suggests a similar idea (p. 140).

31. Tyrus Hillway makes this point in "Taji's Quest for Certainty," *American Literature*, xviii (1946), 27–34.

32. Bernstein argues convincingly that "the major critical point to be made in a discussion of Yillah and Hautia is not so much an exact definition of what they symbolize, for this, in my opinion, is impossible, but to show that Yillah and Hautia are in the long run inseparable, different sides of the same coin, so to speak" (p. 36).

The beautiful heralds who follow Taji may be Hautia's agents of corrupt seduction, but their flowers and their gentleness provoke thoughts of Yillah. On the other hand, the sons of Aleema are part of the Yillah story because they are attempting to avenge her kidnapping and the death of their father. Yet they are dangerous and to be avoided at all costs, and thus suggest Hautia with whom they have no logical tie. Whenever the avengers appear, the heralds cannot be far behind and vice-versa. After the death of Aleema his sons are heard of again for the first time in Chapter 100, and that same evening (Chapter 101) the heralds appear. After news comes that the pursuers have killed Jarl, the heralds again appear the same evening. When Taji and his friends are leaving the Isle of Fossils, the avengers narrowly miss Taji with their arrows. Immediately following this incident Hautia's heralds approach them. In the woods of Diranda Taji is wounded in the arm by an arrow from one of the avengers. When they look for the sons of Aleema, they find instead the heralds. Thus the encounters go, time and again, establishing a pattern in which the avengers and the heralds are mingled, foreshadowing in the end the fading of Yillah into Hautia.

Ordinarily unity signifies harmony, and cycles suggest evolutionary progress, as in Emerson's thought. The pessimism of *Mardi* is of the most distressing sort because unity results only in ambiguity and cycles mean merely endless repetition. Circular imagery permeates *Mardi*, and wherever it is found, it supports the book's theme of eternal and meaningless cyclic movement. Quoting Bardianna, Babbalanja expresses this idea: "Wherefore, it is a perpetual cycling with us, without progression; and we fly round, whether we will or no. To stop, were to sink into space. So, over and over we go, and round and round; double-shuffle, on our axis, and round the sun. . . . There is neither apogee nor perigee, north nor south, right nor left; what to-night is our zenith, to-morrow is our nadir" (p. 460).

The image of the whirlpool is probably the best single indicator in the book of the perniciousness of circles and cycles. It is mentioned first in Chapter 36 when Annatoo is struck on the forehead and is "swallowed up in the whirlpool under our lea" (p. 117). Near the end Taji and his friends narrowly escape death when a great maelstrom forms near them and drags down a thousand small boats and their occupants (p. 586). Aleema intended to sacrifice Yillah in the whirlpool of Tedaidee, and she becomes convinced that "the whirlpool . . . prefigured her fate; that in the waters she saw lustrous eyes, and beckoning phantoms, and strange shapes smoothing her a couch among the mosses" (p. 159). Shortly before she disappears, she has nightmares about it. The whirlpool on Hautia's island is a projection of Hautia—she speaks of herself as "the vortex that draws all in" (p. 650). When Taji arrives on Flozella, it becomes clear that the whirlpool of Yillah's dreams is inseparable from Hautia, who has somehow engulfed Yillah and now invites Taji to dive deeply within the vortex for all he seeks. Taji escapes Hautia in one sense, but he is nevertheless caught up forever in the whirlpool of his endless circuitous search.

If _Mardi_ is Melville's most tedious work of fiction, it is partly because its every aspect illustrates this theme. _Everything_ in the book goes "round and round." Circles upon circles occur from the first pages onward. In the first chapter "the days went slowly round and round, endless and uneventful as cycles in space" (p. 5). Jarl's freckles are described as "symmetrically circular," and Jarl himself is like "a wheel in a machine which forever goes round, whether you look at it or no" (p. 35). In the water the fish "seemed to swim by revolving round and round . . . like a wheel" and "with the round horizon for an arena" (p. 42). A sea-gull makes great concentric circles, "as if an asteroid had fallen into the brine" (p. 49). From the time when Taji and Jarl desert the _Arcturion_ they travel undeviatingly westward as if determined to circle the globe. When they reach Odo they find it "a little round world" (p. 190), as indeed the entire archepelago of Mardi is. On their circular journey among the islands of Mardi they encounter such rulers as Peepi, in whom there are many souls "revolving": Donjalolo, whose House of the Morning is at "the center of many circumferences"

(p. 239); Borabolla, who is "round all over; round of eye and of head; and like the jolly round Earth, roundest and biggest about the Equator" (p. 285); and King Rondo the Round. Many of the islands they visit are round, as is Nora-Bamma. Meanwhile much conversation takes place among the travelers about circles. Babbalanja says that "backward or forward, eternity is the same; already have we been the nothing we dread to be" (p. 237), and he theorizes that it is safer to be in the center of a circle than on the circumference (p. 475). Later "they sail round an island without landing; and talk round a subject without getting at it" (p. 491). Taji has a dream in which he is revolving "round the great central Truth, sun-like" (p. 368), and on Serenia, Babbalanja dreams that "we lighted on a ring, circling a space, where mornings seemed forever dawning over worlds unlike" (p. 633).

The point of this profusion of circle imagery is apparently to make it painfully clear that the circle is the most infernal of signs and as such best represents the nature of things. When Babbalanja accuses Mardians of "essaying our best to square" the circle (p. 457), he is charging the human race with blindness. Later he relates a tale about a philosopher named Grando who had "a sovereign contempt for his carcass." Not realizing that body and mind are one, Grando so abuses his body that he paralyzes himself and is found dead one morning under a tree. Babbalanja's conclusion is that Grando "was intent upon squaring the circle" (pp. 505–506).

Ironically Babbalanja himself later attempts to square the circle on Serenia, as his dream of a place "where mornings seemed forever dawning" indicates. References to the rising sun appear frequently in *Mardi* but never to signify hope or progress. Babbalanja dreams of perpetual dawning, but if the sun rises it also sets. And in a universe of continual movement and change, where nothing is permanent nor stable, neither is there anything new. It is precisely as the writer of Ecclesiastes stated it:

Vanity of vanities; all is vanity. . . . One generation passeth away, and another generation cometh: but the earth abideth for ever. The sun also ariseth, and the sun goeth down, and hasteth to his place where he arose. The wind goeth toward the south, and turneth about unto the north; it whirleth about continually, and the wind returneth again according to his circuits. All the rivers run into the sea; yet the sea is not full: unto the place from whence the rivers come, thither they return again. . . . The thing that hath been, it is that which shall be; and that which is done is that which shall be done: and there is no new thing under the sun. (1:2, 4–7, 9)

Echoes of this passage from Ecclesiastes reverberate throughout *Mardi*. Babbalanja tells the poet Yoomy, "All vanity, vanity," to see in the cyclic processes of nature the answer to higher aspirations (p. 210), and a few pages later Taji says: "For to make an eternity, we must build with eternities; whence, the vanity of the cry for any thing alike durable and new" (pp. 228–29). In commenting on King Donjalolo's two palaces—the House of the Morning and the House of the Afternoon—Taji again sounds like the preacher of Ecclesiastes: "Thus with life: man bounds out of night; runs and babbles in the sun; then returns to his darkness again; though, peradventure, once more to emerge" (p. 233). In the next chapter Babbalanja cries out in agony that "nothing abideth; the river of yesterday floweth not to-day; the sun's rising is a setting; living is dying; the very mountains melt; and all revolve:—systems and asteroids; the sun wheels through the zodiac, and the zodiac is a revolution. Ah gods! in all this universal stir, am *I* to prove one stable thing?" (pp. 237–38).[33] Again using the rising and setting of the sun as his chief image, Babbalanja later echoes the preacher's words that "there is no new thing under the sun": "All we discover has been with us since the sun began to roll. . . . Tell us, ye sages! something worth an archangel's learning; discover, ye discoverers, something new. Fools, fools! Mardi's not changed: the sun yet rises in its old place in the East . . ." (p. 580).

The cycle suggested by these passages based on Ecclesiastes be-

33. Nathalia Wright, in *Melville's Use of the Bible* (Durham, 1949), notes the similarity between Ecclesiastes and this passage from *Mardi* (pp. 97–98). See also Bernstein, pp. 39–40.

comes strongly impressed upon the reader's mind through continual references in *Mardi* to the passing of day into night and
night into morning. Nearly a third of the 195 chapters begins with
some mention of the time of day in the first or second sentence.
The opening lines of Chapters 169–174 illustrate this pattern:
"Morning dawned upon the same mild, blue Lagoon . . ." (p. 556);
"By noon, down came a calm" (p. 558); "Next morning, we came
to a deep, green wood . . ." (p. 562); "That afternoon was melting
down to eve . . ." (p. 565); "Now suns rose, and set; moons grew,
and waned . . ." (p. 567); ". . . No sadness on this merry morn!"
(p. 569). Elsewhere chapters begin with such sentences as "Five
suns rose and set" (p. 160); or "The day was waning" (p. 582); or
"Night and morn departed" (p. 588); or "Life or death, weal or
woe, the sun stays not his course" (p. 615).[34] The effect of such
references to the passing of time is mere empty repetition, for the
cycle of day and night, which Melville makes the reader so conscious of, signifies nothing in a circular journey that will never end
for a narrator who can never die.

34. Nature's cyclic processes are also illustrated by frequent references to
alternating storms and calms.

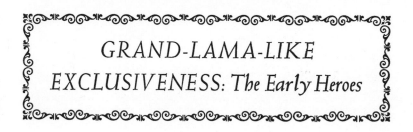

GRAND-LAMA-LIKE
EXCLUSIVENESS: The Early Heroes

Chapter 7

The heroes of Melville's first five books are, of course, different characters, but they can also be viewed as the same man represented in different stages of life. Thus a composite portrait of Melville's tragic hero emerges. Sensitive and restless, he leaves home as a youth, hungry for experience. He stumbles, feels isolated and lonely, and yearns for some past happiness, but finally begins to understand something of the nature of life. He sees that the world is a "moving world" and that there are really no dogmas or guidelines that infallibly explain life. He must, therefore, cast out into the uncertainty and insecurity of fresh experience and deep, earnest thought. He begins to see the necessity of *being*, of existing within himself, of remaining, in a word, independent—or at least as independent as possible. At that stage in his progression he is a solitary restless wanderer. He never feels sufficiently independent, however. Psychologically the hunger for independence is insatiable and thus ultimately destructive. As the fire burns it feeds upon itself, and the more intense it burns the surer its destruction. The extreme state of independence is apotheosis. At that point the hero reaches his greatest stature as a man because he has transcended human dependency; and, simultaneously and paradoxically, he ceases to be a man.

In the pursuit of psychological freedom Melville's early heroes must confront a variety of dangerous entanglements, some temptingly sweet, such as family ties and dogmas of many kinds (the easy answers of the lee shore), some menacingly evil, from the obvious corruption of a Jackson to the captivating degeneracy of a Long Ghost, from the naked ugliness of Liverpool to the plush depravity of Aladdin's Palace. The most subtle threat to the hero's independence, however, is the phenomenon of time.

Melville's consciousness of time's tyranny amounted to almost a preoccupation. His use of the subject is perhaps most apparent in *Pierre* with the recurrent metaphors of chronometer and horologe and with frequent outcries of frustration: "Oh, what quenchless feud is this, that Time hath with the sons of Men!"[1] In the first five novels time is the mirror of character and molder of structure.

As the hero moves toward apotheosis, his response to time changes, and since all five novels are narrated in the first person, this changing reaction to time becomes an essential aspect of Melville's technical art. For example, Melville's first book creates a sense of the widest disparity of any of the five novels between the time of the events of the story and the time they are related by the narrator, Tommo. It is not that Tommo has changed so drastically since he lived with the Typees. Indeed, he has not essentially changed at all. The distinct sense of separation between present and past in *Typee*, between Tommo "then" and Tommo "now," results from the gradual revelation that he is still trying to retreat to the past; he has not learned to be independent of it. He is, in fact, enslaved by it. The more a man lives in the past, the wider the gap seems to his listeners between his past and the present. The more independent a narrator is of the past, the narrower seems the breach

1. *Pierre*, ed. Henry A. Murray (New York, 1949), p. 7.

between the time of the events he is recounting and the moment he is speaking.

With *Redburn* there is actually a greater difference between the narrator and the protagonist, the man who tells the story and his younger self who is the hero of that story. Through tone the narrator makes it clear how much he has matured since his voyage to Liverpool when he was "then but a boy." He frequently makes fun of his Sunday school attitudes and boyish naiveté. Despite the greater actual time span than that in *Typee*, the past does not seem as distant. The reason is that Redburn has learned something about the past that Tommo did not know. He has had enough experience to reveal the truth of Heraclitus's observation that flux is the nature of life, that one never puts his foot twice in the same river. Redburn's revelation about his father's guidebook of Liverpool and his resultant awareness that the world is a *moving* world free him to a large measure from the bondage of the past.

The hero thus makes progress toward independence from time, with the first important stage in that movement the dominance of present over past. In *White-Jacket* the gap between past and present becomes still narrower. White-Jacket relates his past actions and observations with great clarity. It is much easier to see what he has seen and done while a sailor aboard the *Neversink* than it is to tell what he has been. The inner portrait of the younger White-Jacket is filled out largely through indirection, through such devices as the double to project concretely what the narrator was like in the past. White-Jacket realizes much more clearly than Tommo and even more keenly than Redburn the danger which the past represents to man's independence of thought. "The Past is, in many things, the foe of mankind," he says. "In the Past is no hope. . . . The Past is the text-book of tyrants." And he seems to be describing Tommo when he says, "Those who are solely governed by the Past stand like Lot's wife, crystallized in the act of looking backward, and forever incapable of looking before" (p. 150).

White-Jacket is still somewhat deceived about time, however.

If he has learned painfully to break the shackles of the past, the future holds him in its grip. He is Melville's reformer. The injustices in naval life can and should be righted, he repeats. The world of the future can be a much better place. In the same passage where he recognizes the tyranny of the past he says: "The Future is endowed with such a life, that it lives to us even in anticipation. . . . The Future is, in all things, our friend. . . . The Future is both hope and fruition. . . . The Future [is] the Bible of the Free" (p. 150). Tommo, Redburn, and White-Jacket all conceive of time as a linear process consisting of the past, the present, and the future. For Tommo the future is unbearable, the present insufferable; so he tries to move backward in time and recapture something he never really had. White-Jacket knows the past is dead, but he looks toward the future as if it were some glowing landmark ahead on a straight but difficult road.

Time in *Omoo* seems almost suspended. In the plot the passage of time is relatively unimportant. Nor is time a factor in the point of view. In *Typee, Redburn,* and *White-Jacket* the span of time between events and the telling of them is sensed to varying degrees. In *Omoo* the narrator and the protagonist have become one. No distinction is created between what the narrator once was and now is. Unlike Tommo he is not yearning to return to a past he now thinks was beautiful. He does not articulate, as Redburn so clearly does, how his outlook on life has changed since the events he narrates. Apparently it has not changed. He lives neither in the past nor for the future. In this novel Melville's brightest and most optimistic, a happy equilibrium in the hero is apparent. He has no problems with time. Gladly rid of his own past, he refuses to question the past of his closest companion, Long Ghost. He gives little thought to the future, which is as unreal to him as the past. He does not deny the reality of linear time, of the past and the future, but it is only the present which is truly meaningful to him. *Omoo* is only an interlude, however, for the hero of Melville's fiction cannot remain long in this intermediate state of being— having come far enough to feel comparatively free of linear (or human) time, but not far enough yet to feel caught inextricably in circular (or cosmic) time.[2]

It is in *Mardi* that the hero reaches that final stage. With apotheosis comes vision (if not acceptance). Taji and Ahab rebel stronger and blaspheme louder as they perceive the impossibility of complete freedom from cosmic time. Taji declares that he is his "own soul's emperor" (p. 654). Ahab proclaims no one his master—"Talk not to me of blasphemy, man; I'd strike the sun if it insulted me."[3] Madness, which is divinest truth in Melville, is inevitable for these Promethean heroes because they want nothing so much as total and absolute independence, but just when it appears that they have broken out of time, they find themselves caught in a vast unending circle. When Taji transcends human limitations through supreme exertion of the will, he ought to feel free, like a god, but instead his new vision, a vision of cosmic things, reveals an eternal circular course for him. The twelve places named in the book which Taji and his companions visit could be the twelve numbers on the face of a clock.

The concept of time which emerges from *Mardi* could thus be described as frustrating repetition. Time is only movement, and movement is eternally circular—a dog chasing its tail. Melville brilliantly develops a difficult and abstract idea through his creation of a point of view that must be the most ambitious attempt

2. Melville's treatment of this subject is not an effort to define the actual nature of time so much as it is a way of showing how his characters conceive of the phenomenon. In this area, as in all other areas, Melville would not himself pretend definite and final knowledge. Man cannot make statements about what is but only about what he alone perceives: a man *is* what and how he sees. No single writer opens more doors to Melville's way of thinking than the modern German philosopher Edmund Husserl, who wrote that "One cannot discover the least trace of Objective time through phenomenological analysis" (*The Phenomenology of Internal Time-Consciousness*, ed. Martin Heidegger, trans. James S. Churchill, Bloomington, 1964, p. 24) and "we must not make assertions about that which we do not ourselves *see* (*The Paris Lectures*, trans. Peter Koestenbaum, The Hague, 1964, p. 9).

3. *Moby-Dick*, p. 144.

of that age in the technique of narration. In the same moment of time—the point of narration—the past, present, and future are all suggested. Concurrently the narrator is a sailor telling his earthly adventures and a demigod doomed to eternal circularity. Georges Poulet's penetrating description of Ahab's fate could be applied with equal validity to Taji: "The horror of Ahab's destiny consists not in his being lost with all his crew, but in his having to begin the pursuit all over again after his death, only to find a new engulfment awaiting him at the end of this new quest."[4]

Apotheosis is thus the final and greatest paradox. Those predestined for this martyrdom grow in stature as they sail perilously in the howling infinite. But the closer they get to truth, the farther away it is. The more they perceive, the narrower becomes their vision. The more they crave perfection, the more they contribute to imperfection. As they become independent of the forces that debase and enslave ordinary mortals, they are caught up in the insidiousness of cosmic circularity, never to be released. The more they become like a god, the greater their capacity for suffering. The story of Pip, the cabin boy in *Moby-Dick*, is a paradigm of the hero's "ocean-perishing" and apotheosis. After he jumps from a boat, Pip is left alone for several minutes in the open sea. When he is finally picked up, he is mad. His madness is the result of feeling the loneliness which the searching hero inevitably experiences:[5] "But the awful lonesomeness is intolerable. The intense concentration of self in the middle of such a heartless immensity, my God! who can tell it?" Accompanying this intensified loneliness and contributing to his madness is a vision of the inner workings of the universe. He was "carried down alive to wondrous depths, where strange shapes of the unwarped primal world glided to and fro before his passive eyes; and the miser-merman, Wisdom,

4. *Studies in Human Time*, trans. Elliott Coleman (Baltimore, 1956), p. 341.

5. Pip is not himself a searching hero, of course. What happens to him, however, is described in language which applies to such heroes as Taji and Ahab.

revealed his hoarded heaps; and among the joyous, heartless, ever-juvenile eternities, Pip saw the multitudinous, God-omnipresent, coral insects, that out of the firmament of waters heaved the colossal orbs. He saw God's foot upon the treadle of the loom, and spoke it; and therefore his shipmates called him mad. So man's insanity is heaven's sense."[6]

Literally Pip perhaps sees some form of coral when he goes under the water. Symbolically it is the vision which awaits such heroes as Taji and Ahab in apotheosis. From diving deeply into the howling infinite, as Ishmael says in "The Lee Shore," one's humanity perishes, but from the experience comes such knowledge as only the gods possess. The creation of coral (and especially of a coral reef) "out of the firmament of waters" suggests the creation of the universe and the repetitious activity of those "multitudinous, God-omnipresent" forces that have continued since creation.[7] The heart of the vision, however, is *what* they have created—the "colossal orbs"—merely circles upon circles upon circles.[8]

The state of independence which Melville's hero finally reaches produces three closely related attitudes in him: (1) He pays little attention to the laws and dogmas of the world which ordinary people follow; they are generally beneath his consideration, and he does not act as he does to obey laws or because he is afraid of punishment if he breaks them. (2) He has developed a singleness

6. *Moby-Dick*, p. 347.

7. The coral polyps engage in a strange and wonderful form of creativity as they take from the "firmament" of the sea calcium carbonate and turn it into pure limestone, which is deposited to make their own circular (or tubular) shells and hence the circular coral reefs.

8. For a perceptive treatment of Pip's experience as well as the phenomenon of time in Melville, see Paul Brodtkorb, Jr., *Ishmael's White World: A Phenomenological Reading of Moby-Dick* (New Haven, 1965). Brodtkorb and I disagree, however, on the issue of transcending time. While it is my contention that in Melville's works the hero cannot, even through madness, break out of time, Brodtkorb maintains that "descent, unlike ascent, can finally break the chain of time, process, and circular motion. . . . In the end, successfully to escape circular horizontality is either to die or to go mad" (p. 41).

of purpose which frees his conscience of pangs which an ordinary man might feel. Ahab, for example, is not guilt-ridden because he has to commit certain acts against humanity. To Taji also, all things are subordinate to the central pursuit. (3) Consequently such heroes feel free to make use of the world around them in any way that will help them to be about their appointed task.

These three characteristics of psychological freedom follow precisely the three "parts" of true "liberty" which John Calvin discussed and analyzed in his *Institutes of the Christian Religion.* First, "believers ... must rise above the law," he wrote, "and think no more of obtaining justification by it. For while the law ... leaves not one man righteous, we are either excluded from all hope of justification, or we must be loosed from the law. . . ."[9] Secondly, "the soul must previously be divested of every other thought and feeling" except love of God, and "*all its powers collected and united on this one object*" (italics mine).[10] If this is truly done, one's conscience is not encumbered with petty guilts and regrets. Finally, "the third part of this liberty is, that we are not bound before God to any observance of external things which are in themselves indifferent, but that we are now at full liberty either to use or omit them. The knowledge of this liberty is very necessary to us; where it is wanting our consciences will have no rest. . . ."[11] Knowingly or not, Melville was using a Calvinistic framework to arrive at his own unique final vision (which is anything but Calvinistic).

This tragic vision of man in the howling infinite owes a great deal in several other respects—perhaps more than Melville would have cared to admit—to the teachings of Calvin. Melville was brought up and baptized in the Dutch Reformed Church. Although he rejected its dogma (as he did every other kind) and at times reacted strongly against its narrowness, it was neverthe-

9. *Institutes of the Christian Religion,* trans. Henry Beveridge (London, 1953), II, 131.

10. Ibid., II, 133.

11. Ibid., II, 134.

less one of the most important influences of his youth.[12] His specific beliefs about God are more difficult to pin down than the exact meanings of the white whale he created; it is probably just as wrong to view him as an orthodox Calvinist as it is to see him as a bitter and consistent God-hater. He may not have believed in Calvinism at all, but what he *did* believe—as reflected in the first five novels—bears enough resemblance to Calvin's theology as to suggest its derivation from that system of religious thought "from whose visitations, in some shape or other," he wrote, "no deeply thinking mind is always and wholly free."[13]

Melville's deep respect for the howling infinite puts him in the company of all those who admire Christian's journey through such obstacles as the Slough of Despond and the Valley of Humiliation. It smacks of the Calvinistic ideal of noble hardship. That which is comfortable and easy—whether it be Typee or Vanity Fair—must be avoided, for suffering, not complacency or contentment, is the true catalyst for man's growth. Melville was in sympathy with Hawthorne's viewpoint in "The Celestial Railroad," where a fast new train bypasses all difficulties on the way to heaven —and consequently never gets there.

What Melville derived from Calvin was not a religious belief so much as an understanding of basic human nature and a sense of man's perilous position in life—his destiny having been largely decided for him. Oddly enough, one of the most systematized of

12. For discussions of this influence, see Newton Arvin, *Herman Melville* (New York, 1950); William Braswell, *Melville's Religious Thought* (Durham, 1943), William H. Gilman, *Melville's Early Life and Redburn* (New York, 1951), Lawrance Thompson, *Melville's Quarrel with God* (Princeton, 1952), and Yvor Winters, *Maule's Curse* (Norfolk, Conn., 1938). A recent treatment of Melville's indebtedness in *Moby-Dick* to certain concepts of Calvinism is T. Walter Herbert, Jr., "Calvinism and Cosmic Evil in *Moby-Dick*," *PMLA*, LXXXIV (1969), 1613-19. Herbert's focus is different from my own: he argues that Ahab is Calvin's "reprobate" attacking the Calvinistic God.

13. "Hawthorne and His Mosses," in *Billy Budd and Other Prose Pieces* (London, 1924), p. 129.

dogmas—Calvinism—may have also taught Melville that dogmas are entirely inadequate to explain the riddle of the universe. There is something profoundly mysterious and unfathomable about the Calvinistic God who allows evil to flourish and who predestines men according to some pattern known only to Himself. Calvin cautioned that man could never really understand God. Similarly Melville believed that God, or whatever it was that had its "foot on the treadle of the loom," could not be deciphered.

The central tenet of Calvin's theology was the doctrine of the elect. It separated all mankind into two broad categories—the favored and the damned. There was no use trying to decide *why* this should be or, after discovering its reality, to "throw bricks at the temple," as Stephen Crane would say. "Because God of his mere good pleasure," wrote Calvin, "electing some passes by others, they raise a plea against him. But if the fact is certain, what can they gain by quarrelling with God? . . . Let them tell why men are better than oxen or asses. God might have made them dogs [instead of men]. . . ."[14] Those who are among the elect, taught Calvin, are born with a mysterious protection against the corrosive acid of evil. Satan can go only so far with them and then no further, for despite their tendency to sin—their "depravity"—their immortal souls are untouchable. The damned, however, cannot be saved because that essence of Godliness has been left out of their makeup. It is almost as if God, in Calvin's scheme, had created a true race of human beings in his own image and another race that resembled human beings but were greatly different—as different as wolves from lambs or androids from men—because they did not possess the deep goodness of heart that is divine.

No matter how vigorously Melville rejected the creeds of his Calvinist upbringing, he could not get around the idea that men are what they are and that some are evil to the core while others— the Jack Chases and the Mad Jacks of the world—are indelibly marked with their basic decency. To preach goodness to some

14. *Institutes of the Christian Religion*, II, 213.

men, Melville knew, was as futile as the cook Fleece preaching restraint and brotherhood to the sharks in *Moby-Dick*. There was no possibility for change in men like Jackson or Babo. Melville would have agreed with F. Scott Fitzgerald that "a sense of the fundamental decencies is parcelled out unequally at birth."[15]

All five of Melville's early heroes have this fundamental decency. In fact, they seem as innately incorruptible as Calvin's elect.[16] When one is tempted to lead an easy but stagnant existence, he is in agony until he can return to the hard life of the sea. Melville's youngest hero leaves home at a tender age and is exposed to an almost endless variety of the world's evils but remains inviolable. Another reaches manhood and retains his soul while aboard a navy man-o-war, amid "the pent-up wickedness of five hundred men." Still another hero is given a rich opportunity to become a permanent beachcomber, but even while he is temporarily pursuing that life with an appealing reprobate companion, his honor and seriousness are never in question. And, finally, the hellish fate that lies in store for Taji is ironically the result of his love of perfection and purity rather than a mark of any innate corruption.

These heroes are members of Melville's true church of the elect. When he speaks in *Omoo* (and elsewhere) of the difference between a true sailor and one who simply bears the name of sailor, he is speaking of the innate difference in men much as Calvin did when he distinguished between the visible and invisible church. Melville's true sailor may be compared to the member of the invisible church, "into which none are admitted but those who by the gift of adoption are sons of God . . . all the elect who have existed from the beginning of the world."[17] The sailor in name only is like Calvin's churchmember in name only, who participates

---

15. *The Great Gatsby* (New York, 1953), p. 1.

16. By "incorruptible" I do not mean to imply saintliness. Tommo and Taji, for example, both find it necessary to take the life of another human being. When the hero commits an evil, however, it is always without giving the sense of *being* evil.

17. *Institutes of the Christian Religion*, II, 288.

in all the rituals of the visible church but who is eternally outside the circle of the elect. "In this [the visible] church," he said, "there is a very large mixture of hypocrites, who have nothing of Christ but the name and outward appearance: of ambitious, avaricious, envious, evil-speaking men, some also of impurer lives, who are tolerated for a time, either because their guilt cannot be legally established, or because due strictness of discipline is not always observed. Hence, as it is necessary to believe the invisible Church, which is manifest to the eye of God only, so we are also enjoined to regard this Church which is so called with reference to man...."[18]

For Calvin's elect the way, curving and rocky though it may be, leads to salvation and eternal joy. For Melville's elect the way leads to frustration. Diametrically opposed as these views are, the development of Melville's tragic hero from restless young wanderer to mad searcher is made up of stages somewhat like those described by Calvin: "In regard to the elect, we regard calling as the evidence of election, and justification as another symbol of its manifestation, until it is fully accomplished by the attainment of glory. But as the Lord seals his elect by calling and justification, so by excluding the reprobate either from the knowledge of his name or the sanctification of his Spirit, he by these marks in a manner discloses the judgment which awaits them."[19] The tragic hero of Melville, incorruptible as he is and thus distinguished from the reprobate, is "called," is compelled to lead a certain kind of life and is made aware of his specialness as a man and his need for independence in order to be, in a sense, about his father's business, which is the pursuit of truth. His attainment of "glory" is apotheosis, not spiritual salvation in the Christian sense, but nevertheless a state which is not ordinarily human either.

Melville's first five novels, then, form a saga of spiritual quest which in some ways resembles *Pilgrim's Progress*. One of the most difficult of Christian's tasks is to give up his family and strike out

18. Ibid.
19. Ibid., p. 211.

alone.[20] So it is with the young hero in Melville. For both the way is lonely and difficult. Both encounter corrupt acquaintances ready to lead them astray and men who through example encourage and teach them. In the end both perish in the water and achieve apotheosis. What glorification means to Melville, however, is far different from its meaning in Bunyan. When Taji is transformed through apotheosis into a demigod, the metamorphosis is not cause for rejoicing, for there is no peace in Melville's eternity.

20. This was the aspect of Christian's journey which struck Mark Twain's wandering hero, Huck Finn, most forcefully. The book, he explained, was "about a man that left his family, it didn't say why." See the Hillcrest Edition of *The Writings of Mark Twain* (New York, 1904), XIII, 141.

EPILOGUE

After Taji sets out with four companions on his prolonged search for Yillah, he eventually discovers that he is accompanied by an elusive fifth character. Along with Babbalanja, Yoomy, Mohi, and Media is a strange, wild, somewhat sardonic personality named Azzageddi, who resides within the complex mind of Babbalanja, a kind of second self. In Babbalanja's discourse on personal devils (Chapter 104) he suggests that all men are to some extent "bedeviled," and he gives a hint that his own private demon will later show itself. Later Azzageddi appears repeatedly, sometimes babbling such seeming nonsense as "fugle-fi, fugle-fo, fugle-fogle-orum," sometimes expounding useless (and questionable) information: "Perfect Dicibles are of various sorts: Interrogative; Percontative; Adjurative; Optative; Imprecative; Execrative; Substitutive; Compellative; Hypothetical; and, lastly, Dubious" (pp. 505, 563). He frequently makes profound sense, however, which usually points out the folly of human existence. Irreverent and undaunted, he mocks and sneers at humankind. Wild as he is, he is controllable. When Babbalanja or his companions have had enough of Azzageddi, he can be silenced: "Down, devil! deeper down!" rumbles Babbalanja as he subdues the wild spirit within.

Although Azzageddi is specifically identified only in *Mardi*, he is present in all of Melville's early heroes. He does not represent corruption or evil but that impulse to break away, to be free, to do and say things that ordinary people dare not. He is the howling infinite internalized and personified. It makes no sense to Azzageddi to be merely human. Human life is absurd to him. It is subject to pains and anxieties, limited, finite, fragile. He wants to leap from star to star, soar through the cosmic night, and hear his mad shrieks of unbounded freedom reverberate through the universe. Then he is pushed back, downed; and the logical, rational, and practical forces of life once again assume control. But he will not be denied indefinitely. Whenever he senses the occasion is right, he appears again with an upsurge of emotion, crying for freedom, impatient of restraint, intolerant of manners, rules, and mores.

It is Azzageddi who taunts Tommo until he frees himself from the natives who hold him in friendly captivity. Azzageddi whispers "freedom, freedom" until Tommo is in frantic agony, desperate to run away. It is Azzageddi who takes control of young Redburn when he discovers on the Hudson River steamer that he has insufficient money for passage. "The devil in me then mounted up from my soul," Redburn says in recounting his strange conduct before the collector of tickets, "and spread over my frame, till it tingled at my finger ends" (p. 13). A momentary rebellion occurs within him, and he affronts not only the ticket clerk but also two of the well-fed passengers who are staring at him. He breaks all rules of respect and decorum under this spell and even points his rifle in sardonic humor at one of the fat men, who exclaims in fear that the boy must be crazy. "So I was at that time; for otherwise I know not how to account for my demoniac feelings, of which I was afterward heartily ashamed, as I ought to have been, indeed; and much more than that" (p. 13). When the orderly world closes in and threatens to bind the hero up in the mummy wrappings of mundane life and law, Azzageddi, the wild champion of independence, breaks forth in a fury.

But Azzageddi is also present at other moments, those times when the mind seems to expand and soar. It is Azzageddi that Babbalanja has been listening to when he tells Media: "The thrilling of my soul's monochord, my lord. But prick not your ears to hear it; that divine harmony is overheard by the rapt spirit alone; it comes not by the auditory nerves" (p. 562). Such moments are not uncommon to the early heroes when they are alone in the rigging. "Then was I first conscious," says Redburn, "of a wonderful thing in me, that responded to all the wild commotion of the outer world; and went reeling on and on with the planets in their orbits, and was lost in one delirious throb at the center of the All. A wild bubbling and bursting was at my heart, as if a hidden spring had just gushed out there; and my blood was tingling along my frame, like mountain brooks in spring freshets" (p. 66). It is Azzageddi who lifts White-Jacket to heights of near delirium as he gazes at the stars from aloft, feeling fused "into the universe of things, and . . . a part of the All . . ." (p. 76). He would "die and be glorified" with the stars at that ecstatic moment. But upon his experience of transcendence intrudes the "life in a man-of-war, which, with its martial formalities and thousand vices, stabs to the heart the soul" of Azzageddi (p. 77). It is also Azzageddi who beckons to the hero of *Omoo* to give up the pleasures of Tahiti and return to the infinite sea, which Azzageddi loves for its tempestuous gales, an echo of his own voice. Finally it is Azzageddi who takes control of Taji and carries him, with "eternity . . . in his eye," beyond that outer "barrier" of life (p. 654).

The Azzageddi impulse makes the hero heroic; it is the urge to rise above limitations of flesh and bone and soar over the wall of reason. Although most of the young narrator-heroes express that urge only on occasion, that is enough to make it clear that they are all "bedeviled," as Babbalanja puts it. The hero's movement toward apotheosis is in direct proportion to Azzageddi's growth within him. These first five novels are distinctive as a segment of Melville's total work because Azzageddi is an important force, struggling for recognition in all of them and breaking out in full view in *Mardi*. He then goes on to achieve his greatest power in *Moby-Dick* through Ahab and, in part, Ishmael.

After *Moby-Dick* Azzageddi begins his decline.[1] He is still loudly heard in *Pierre* raving against things as they are, but his rage for freedom there becomes the frustrated cry of something lost, the last desperate complaint of a man about to be executed. His execution is performed by the same force he contends with in the early work—the everyday world made up of common sense, logic, practicality, and, above all, custom. "Such, oh thou son of man!" wrote Melville in *Pierre*, "are the perils and the miseries thou callest down on thee, when, even in a virtuous cause, thou steppest aside from those arbitrary lines of conduct, by which the common world, however base and dastardly, surrounds thee for thy worldly good."[2] In such a world, as Captain Vere believed, "Forms, measured forms, are everything."[3]

The unresolved tension between Azzageddi and order makes for one of the richest aspects of the early novels. It probably resulted chiefly from Melville's personal struggle with the world and his ambiguous feelings about his own Azzageddi. He realized that he had to please the reading public. Even more important, he knew that a writer must keep himself in hand. Art is not all inspiration and hallucination. One side of his nature was appalled when Azzageddi reared his dragon's head and threatened to breathe undisciplined fire into his writings. There must have been times when Melville, seized with the desire to break out, echoed Babbalanja's words: "Fangs off! fangs off! depart, thou fiend!—un-

---

1. Some of my observations about Melville's later heroes parallel those of John Seelye in his *Melville: The Ironic Diagram* (Evanston, 1970). *An Artist in the Rigging* had just been completed when Mr. Seelye's book was published.

2. *Pierre* (New York, 1949), p. 207.

3. *Billy Budd* (Chicago, 1962), p. 128.

hand me! or . . . I will die and spite thee!" (p. 579). Yet he also recognized that Azzageddi emerged untrammeled and pure from the deepest recesses of his soul. Azzageddi was not influenced toward practicality by crying babies or unpaid bills or the thirst for fame. It was Azzageddi speaking within Melville himself when he wrote Hawthorne in 1851 praising "the man who . . . declares himself a sovereign nature (in himself) amid the powers of heaven, hell, and earth. He may perish; but so long as he exists he insists upon treating with all Powers upon an equal basis. If any of those other Powers choose to withhold certain secrets, let them; that does not impair my sovereignty in myself; that does not make me a tributary."[4] This was the noblest impulse, the untainted fire, and when Melville fought and subdued that impulse, as he sometimes did in the early novels, he felt that he had cheated, that he had written for money, had surrendered to materialistic pressures. When that happened, he hated himself and disparaged his work. On the other hand, when he allowed Azzageddi a full rein, as he did through some of *Mardi*, he paid for it by the chastisement of reviewers, by the prospect of imminent poverty, and by the hovering specter of madness.

By the time he finished *Pierre* his frustration was intense—the practical and ordinary world loomed up before him as an insuperable barrier to freedom, personal and artistic. He was writing of himself as well as Pierre when he said: "The wiser and the profounder he should grow, the more and the more he lessened the chances for bread; . . . could he hurl his deep book out of the window, and fall to on some shallow nothing of a novel, composable in a month at the longest, then could he reasonably hope for both appreciation and cash."[5]

In *Pierre* the enemy of Azzageddi thus proves too strong for him. Enceladus, the mythic Azzageddi, has lost his hundred arms and now "despairing of any other mode of wreaking his im-

4. *The Letters of Herman Melville*, ed. Merrell R. Davis and William H. Gilman (New Haven, 1960), pp. 124–25.

5. *Pierre*, p. 359.

mitigable hate, [has] turned his vast trunk into a battering-ram, and hurled his own arched-out ribs again and yet again against the invulnerable" world of the commonplace.[6] He loses to that unassailable force represented by the lawyer in "Bartleby," the world of "eminently *safe*" men, whose "first grand point" is "prudence," the next, "method."[7] In "Bartleby" Azzageddi gives up his blasphemous shrieking against the gods of ordinary life. His rebellion now against the values, routine, and order of Wall Street is passive resistance. Although Azzageddi's voice continued to be heard in such works as "Cock-A-Doodle-Doo!" (1853), "The Lightning-Rod Man" (1854), and "The Bell-Tower" (1855), Melville's main interest seemed to be in the way of the world.

As Herman Melville's obsessive preoccupation with his own role as misfit grew upon him, he became engaged in depicting repeatedly the contrast between "normal" and "abnormal" men. His deepest concern in much of his important later fiction—"Bartleby," "Benito Cereno," *Israel Potter*, *The Confidence Man*, and *Billy Budd*—was not, however, merely to show the absurdity of bourgeois values and the ridiculousness of reasonable men. Indeed, much to his credit, his portrayals of men like the lawyer in "Bartleby," Captain Delano, and Starry Vere, though often colored by biting irony, are not characterized by vindictiveness or bitterness. To the end Melville remained an artist. But his central subject shifted to what he had come to feel was the greatest incongruity of human existence: the infinite gap in communication and understanding between logical and practical men (like Benjamin Franklin in *Israel Potter*), who have kept the world going with their common sense, and men who were born drastically different, men like Bartleby, or Billy Budd, or Herman Melville.

6. Ibid., p. 407.
7. "Bartleby," in *The Piazza Tales* (London, 1923), p. 20.

Index

Characters from Melville's fiction are listed separately and the works in which they appear identified in parentheses and in abbreviated form (T for *Typee*, O for *Omoo*, M-D for *Moby-Dick*, BC for "Benito Cereno," etc.).